The official City of Madison flag design, accepted on April 12, 1962, by two Madison Boy Scouts, Dennis and Richard Stone. *Image courtesy of Alan De Smet.*

MYSTERIOUS
MADISON

UNSOLVED CRIMES, STRANGE CREATURES
& BIZARRE HAPPENSTANCE

NOAH VOSS
FOREWORD BY LINDA GODFREY

Charleston   London

THE
History
PRESS

Published by The History Press
Charleston, SC 29403
www.historypress.net

Front cover: A man rows a boat on Lake Monona, 1894. *WHS-2123*; Madison State Capitol and a blindfolded statue. *Courtesy of Martin Saunders*; A map from 1911, showing West Madison (the capitol is on the right, a large square with a dark X). *WHS-41578*.

Back cover: First three buildings of the University of Wisconsin Madison; North Hall is on on the far right, 1885. *WHS-188*; An F-89 Jet Interceptor stationed at Madison Truax Air Field, Wisconsin. *Courtesy of the United States government*; A view of South Madison in 1909. *WHS-36063*.

First published 2011

Manufactured in the United States

ISBN 978.1.60949.369.1

Library of Congress Cataloging-in-Publication Data

Voss, Noah.
Mysterious Madison : unsolved crimes, strange creatures and bizarre happenstance / Noah Voss.
p. cm.
ISBN 978-1-60949-369-1
1. Madison (Wis.)--Miscellanea. 2. Madison (Wis.)--History--Anecdotes. 3. Haunted places--Wisconsin--Madison. 4. Curiosities and wonders--Wisconsin--Madison. I. Title.
F589.M157V67 2011
977.5'83--dc23
2011030025

Notice: The information in this book is true and complete to the best of our knowledge. It is offered without guarantee on the part of the author or The History Press. The author and The History Press disclaim all liability in connection with the use of this book.

Contents

FOREWORD

Born in Madison and raised there until the age of eight, I grew up steeped in the weird aura of Wisconsin's capital. My dentist's window opened on Capitol Square, and I could see the gold statue of the lady with the badger hat on her head as my teeth were being drilled. At my elementary school, we had to sing an anthem to our city—"My heart is in Madison, M-A-D-I-S-O-N"—along with saying the Pledge of Allegiance. Even though my parents later moved us away, the city had charmed us so deeply that we returned whenever possible. Our hearts really were there.

It was with extra delight, then, that I learned that my friend Noah Voss had written a book devoted to Madison's twilight side, with all the parts that normal history books leave out. Make no mistake, this *is* history—just not the dull kind. Ghosts of early settlers flutter and moan, lake serpents writhe, trance mediums unionize, mob neighborhoods offer legends that no one can refuse. UFOs zip and glow in the Madison skies, ancient effigy mounds persist in their enigmatic animal shapes and a tuberculosis sanatorium engenders more spooky stories than cures. A lion stalks in daylight.

All of these anomalous gems and more demand the reader's full engagement with things that otherwise might escape notice. I urge you to allow Voss's well-researched tales to whisk you around the lesser-known alleys and avenues of Mad Town until you catch the nebulous scent of Madison's true nature. Perhaps you will even find that Madison's telltale heart is now in you.

Linda Godfrey

Wisconsinite Linda Godfrey is the author of Strange Wisconsin, Monsters of Wisconsin *and many other books on strange and eccentric subjects.*

PREFACE

I developed several goals when I was approached to write this book. Mystery lovers will, no doubt, love the mysterious occurrences outlined within these pages at any time of year. I also wrote with the aim of creating a perfect Halloween pairing for the reader, holding only seasonal interest. As I researched and wrote potential entries, a few screamed to my mental movie machine—alone on a dark and stormy October night. I could see a faceless stranger on a nameless street. The storm deafeningly sounds across the city and has driven all but the boldest indoors. The hypnotically repetitive rain is occasionally populated with decaying, dying and once-dry leaves. They leap back to life only when the chilled wind whips. The storm is the perfect cover for the next mystery-in-the-making. Any sounds of screams are softened by the crack of thunder and the drowning of drops. While not all of the mysteries contained herein are dark, there are some that evoke that imagery to me.

The final goal I had with these documented but unexplained reports was for the avid researcher and investigator to be able to use them in his or her own quest for unequivocally quantifiable answers to some of life's greatest questions. No small feats, only big mysteries. Some of these cases are hundreds of years old. Others fall into more recent history of the last few years.

I have traveled through all but a few states in the United States on my own adventures into the unknown. My current perspective has evolved from over two decades of research and investigation, including learning from those with college-level degrees in parapsychology. By now, I must have traveled through thousands of locations with purported unexplained events connected to them, including numerous international destinations. Sometimes I find myself exploring more than twenty states in a single year. I have had the good fortune to have so many travels, creating a variety of life experiences to draw from regarding the mysteries of events and people. I approach any new legend with the goal of keeping an open and objective mind. On one hand, I always take great effort to approach any mystery without my own predisposed assumptions from past experiences. On the other hand, what I have learned in the last few decades has helped me to remain efficient in my research and investigation and even to stay on the side of calculated risk—which side varies from case to case. This is difficult to balance with the important lessons I've learned through investigating so many locations.

Trying to keep from simply substantiating one's own belief system is a difficult task. At the same time, it is nearly impossible to know for sure if one is ever accomplishing said task successfully. This is reminiscent of the observer paradox found in experimental science. The openness to willingly change my stance in the face of new data is something I've always been conscious of. I cling to no one belief so strongly that it blinds me to new information when discovered. During my research and investigation into these mysteries you are about to read, I approached them and disseminated the information in writing in the same vein. I will present the events as neutrally and factually as possible so you might make your own educated decisions. Of course, where I softly include my own perspective, I make clear that it is my own opinion in order to afford those less traveled the opportunity to view the mystery relative to my experiences.

I have called the Madison area home now for over a decade, so it is only fitting that I take the skills I've acquired through my international adventures and apply them to mysteries in Madison. I hope that you not only enjoy your time becoming engrossed in the following mysteries but also pick up where I leave off. Take any constructive motivations you might find inside this book and apply them to getting out there and trying to uncover new clues to the mysteries. If we are lucky, perhaps you'll be the next to find the final clue solving a great local mystery. I hope to read of your successful sleuthing in the local newspaper or hear of your mystery-solving exploits on the radio—maybe even watch your news interview on how you solved it.

Best of luck, and remember, adventures come to the adventuresome.

ACKNOWLEDGEMENTS

I would like to acknowledge the past efforts of Wisconsin-area folklorists, authors, researchers, journalists and investigators such as Charles Brown, Michael Norman, Beth Scott, Don Schmitt, Dennis Boyer, Jay Rath and Jim Aho. In addition, I am grateful to organizations such as APRO (Aerial Phenomena Research Organization) and CUFOS (Center for Unidentified Flying Objects Studies), which were and are composed of and supported by countless passionate individuals. Without all these personal contributions, today's task of explaining the unexplained would be even greater. Their interests in the unknown surely had an impact on developing my own love of mystery long before I put pen to paper.

For more recent support, I have the pleasure of thanking Jennifer Voss, Chad Lewis, John Albrecht, Kevin Less Nelson, Sean Bindley, Todd Roll, Linda Godfrey, Jesse Donahue, Jay Rath, Timothy Good and Brad Steiger. Your contributions to my endeavors, large or small, have been undeniably essential.

Original plat map for Madison, Wisconsin, 1836. *WHS-38589.*

CENTRAL MADISON

Madison was literally drawn into existence in 1836 while still covered in woods and wetland. Still, the land was not without its people. Indigenous people had visited the lakes of the area regularly for thousands of years. The same year Wisconsin became a territory, James Duane Doty was busy buying up the land that would become Madison. A former federal judge, Mr. Doty bought more than one thousand acres of land and quickly had the plat maps completed. Using his extravagant offering of free fur coats along with discounted land, he was able to convince legislators to choose Madison as the new territory capital. Madison was born.

Any new city, village or township is riddled with firsts. The intriguing part of Madison's firsts is how many rest squarely with one family. In 1837, Roseline Peck, along with her husband, established the first inn in Madison. It was completed with the financial help of James Doty on the afternoon of the city's first Fourth of July celebration. While not named Rhythm and Booms yet, the inn drew a crowd of reportedly hundreds to an area that wouldn't be incorporated as a village for another ten years. The festivities were even attended by locals from the Ho Chunk Nation. The evening is described in generous detail in Roseline's writings. It included beef, veal, feather beds and a basket of champagne. Roseline embodied the strong, capable Wisconsin woman. Even with her husband purportedly "incapacitated" and herself seven months pregnant, everything is said to have gone off without a hitch. Folks sang into the evening, and general joy abounded. Roseline would go on to give Madison another big first: firstborn Wisconsonite Victoria Peck came about soon after.

Independence Day celebrations would not always go as smoothly as the first. In 1871, John Betz was manning a cannon at the capitol lawn celebration. When the cannon went off prematurely, John was disfigured and mortally wounded. He survived the incident long enough to be taken to his home at 1036 University Avenue. He passed the next day.

In 1889, William Melvin was disfigured and later died from a cannon blast. He was also working the Fourth of July celebration on the capitol lawn. Mysteriously connecting the two is the address they both called home. Though almost twenty years apart, and no known relation between them, they were both living at 1036 University Avenue at the time of their forceful demises.

Earlier, in 1837, we have another documented mystery in the downtown district born of someone's death. Indeed, even I have my own connections to these ghastly grounds. Though it was more than one hundred years later while attending college in the area, I, too, heard the haunted tales. The spirits of Bascom Hill, the spooks of Science Hall or some other specter in pretty much every other aged building on the University of Wisconsin campus were thought into existence by the solitary student in the dark of night. Perhaps we should start this ghost story with the end of William Nelson in 1837. During his life in Madison, Nelson worked construction on the capitol building. It's believed that Mr. Nelson also holds the distinction of being the first white man to die in Madison.

The rough and tough years went by as they do for any frontier area. In 1846, Madison became incorporated as a village, with a population of 626. Three years later, the University of Wisconsin–Madison was established.

Over the next few decades, speculation grew on the university campus about the source of a ghostly white figure. Though the details had been documented since 1880, the sightings are rumored to have been going on for years. Most thought the restless spirit of William Nelson was to blame for the disturbances. The first documented sighting speaks of an experience had by a restless sleeper in North Hall.

During the time of this ghost story, North Hall was a dorm for men and, as reported in the student newspaper, the *Daily Cardinal*, perhaps home to something more. The story, as relayed through the paper, is that a student on the second floor awoke one night. Upon leaving his room, he entered the long hallway. At the end stood an "apparition in white" that eerily floated about. The student was said to have jumped back into his room and quickly woke his roommate. Even with the roommate's reluctance at becoming the butt of a joke, the two checked the hall. There was nothing there. Safely back in their room, they began to drift back to sleep. They remained asleep

The first three buildings of the University of Wisconsin– Madison. North Hall is on the far right, 1885. *WHS-1885.*

until the door opened and the apparition floated into the room. It would seem that the two roommates were frozen with fear, as they didn't interact with the apparition; nor did the apparition interact with them. It was said to have simply "departed" after a brief moment. Perhaps it had other witnesses to frighten.

The apparition was spotted all over campus in the ensuing nights. Testimony came in of the ghost's "garments of unearthly whiteness" as it was seen "skipping through the halls and vanishing." The furor must have grown to an uncomfortable level for the university because then-president John Bascom put together an investigative committee of faculty members. The plan was laid out: they would spend time in the dormitories and discover the truth for themselves. However, even before the professors could take away certain unsupervised freedoms undoubtedly enjoyed by the students in the dorms, a confession was made. A student, identified by the *Wisconsin State Journal* on October 24, 1888, as Whitney Trousdale, confessed that he "dressed in a bedsheet and romped through the halls." Was this case closed? As far as the faculty was concerned, yes. The committee closed its investigation. Was Whitney an 1800s scapegoat for the university, put up to confession by the university itself? Perhaps he came forward hoping his punishment would be less harsh at the hands of the faculty than from the other students, who may have known of the prank and not appreciated having professors watching over them in their dorms. Perhaps Whitney was the source of one or more of the ghostly sightings, but maybe not all of them. Maybe some part of Mr. Nelson was still around, trying to pass along something to the living. Of course, this is all speculation.

Since William Nelson's death in 1837, Madison's population had grown to more than ten thousand and the University of Wisconsin system was thriving—ghost stories and all. Indeed, the cemetery where Nelson was initially laid to rest was dug up and moved for lack of room. At least two graves were missed and forgotten during this process. That is, until 1918 when, during renovations to the Bascom Hill area in downtown Madison, the two graves were discovered. If you'd like to believe Whitney was not the only possible source of the apparition, take care to note that the graves found in 1918 were not moved, nor were the remains disinterred. William Nelson and Samuel Warren remain there today, at the feet of the Lincoln statue. The two graves are on the south side and are distinguished with one metal marker each. I'm told that the old North Hall Dormitory still stands today; however, it now houses various offices. It is also likely that the two Independence Day cannon victims were initially laid to rest in the cemetery on Bascom Hill. Both physical remains are entombed today in Forest Hill Cemetery. If anything less than physical remains, might it be roaming the area to this day?

Anyone who has traveled to downtown Madison may easily remember the countless lakes he or she crissed and crossed to arrive. One of these, Lake Mendota, is the scene of our next mystery. The lake dominates the land from the central downtown area to the southeast. Its surface covers 9,740 acres and plunges to a depth of eighty-three icy feet. Large bodies of water have always drawn a part of the population to their edges to imagine what lies beneath. With almost twenty-two miles of shoreline, Lake Mendota has space for many to seek serpents. That's right, lake monsters! Our minds have an uncanny ability to comprehend something right in front of us that is vast and visible yet holds much hidden from view. Large bodies of water are a perfect example. Some individuals are drawn farther than the shoreline and out into the monster-infested waters. We must go back to the 1860s, when W.J. Park and his wife were just this type of brave individual.

Lake Mendota, the very same lake where witnesses watched the serpent, 2011. *Photograph by Noah Voss.*

According to Jay Rath's book *The W-Files*, while boating on Lake Mendota, the Parks drew near Governor's Island and what they took at first to be a log. Upon raising one of their oars to inspect the log, the water began to churn, and the "log" dove down deeper into the water.

Jay quotes W.J. Park as later writing, "This was a monster of some sort, we have no doubt…and we were not too long in deciding that retreat was the better part of valor and we resolved to say nothing about the matter." Keeping quiet proved difficult for W.J. Park and his wife, as the sightings, while they may have started with them, did not end there.

July in Wisconsin brings many things. The days bring high temperatures trumped only by tangible humidity. Today, driveway fireworks displays give way to the city's explosive finale. In 1892, the next documented serpent sighting shocked onlookers. This one was spotted by two people on Lake Monona. The monster quickly moved through the water toward Ott's Springs and Esther Beach. According to *The W-Files* book, Darwin Boehmer and a friend watched the serpent "undulating in an up and down motion" from about seventy-five feet away. In fact, there were people on the shore who witnessed this mysterious creature at the same time. With the lake covering 3,274 acres, it is lucky there were other folks nearby to substantiate the sighting. The nature of the unexplained and mysterious is their seemingly patternless and fleeting appearances that do not always allow for multiple witnesses—a fact most investigators struggle with often and relish when more witnesses can be found. In this case, more witnesses were to be made.

A man rows a boat on Lake Monona, 1894. *WHS-2123.*

Only two months later, Joe Daubner reported "the creature's" location again on Lake Monona. Perhaps a more colorful account of the Lake Monona serpent comes from an anonymous man visiting from Oregon. Jay Rath documents that the creature passed underneath the rowboat rented recently for a day of fishing.

Lake Monona has a maximum depth of sixty-six feet, allowing for plenty of room for the creature, no matter its girth. The witness's story goes on to say the serpent was twenty feet in length and had a large flat-topped head. Quickly rowing back to shore, in the very next moment the witness "vowed never to return to the city without a Winchester rifle and two revolvers." Beyond that, the witness shared that he wouldn't "go back out onto that lake for all the money in the capital city."

The shoreline was not enough for "a number of young men" on November 3, 1892. They, too, found themselves in a boat coming face-to-serpent, according to the *New North*. Thanks to the efforts of author Chad Lewis in his work *The Hidden Headlines of Wisconsin*, we have many of these original newspaper stories reprinted for posterity. The newspapers of the time had the "young men" estimating the size as between twenty-five and thirty-five feet long. A colorful closing was printed: "Not being on a hunt for the serpent they had no firearms and were glad to escape from the monster." Had they weapons, perhaps they might have shot what ended up being an unusually large but poorly estimated muskie or northern pike. These two species of fish are most likely the largest inhabiting any of the lakes surrounding Madison. I personally would find it hard to believe that these early Madison frontiersman would have misidentified anything normally found in these lakes. The 1800s afforded many hardships forgotten in today's comfort, but one thing generally accepted is the people's close relationship to nature and their immediate environment. The day-to-day chores of seeking food from the lakes, rivers, fields and forests would have made many people familiar with the things living there. Those who sought game and goods from the wild—not for food, but for pay—would also have had many experiences with wildlife. Even those simply moving about their daily lives would not have been separated from nature with glass, steel and fifty-five-mile-per-hour speeds. With no further description of said serpent, we may never know exactly what was witnessed.

Perhaps you've noted that the creature sightings have been on Lake Mendota and Lake Monona—so far. The names sound similar, and even many locals will have trouble telling you which one they are in front of at any one time. The two lakes link together at the Yahara River, so any creatures,

A section of the Yahara River, looking north into Lake Mendota, 2011. *Photograph by Noah Voss.*

known or otherwise, would be able to move freely between the lakes without ever leaving the water. In fact, the river itself was subject to its own terrifying serpent sighting about 1892. Thanks again to Jay Rath and his book *The W-Files*, I can share with you that a young man witnessed what "looked like a log, except that it swam and dove—and tried to overturn his boat."

On April 11, 1897, a new mystery was being discussed by the almost nineteen thousand Madison residents. Dubbed the "Great Airship Mystery" by people of the time, it was the modern equivalent of an unidentified flying object (UFO). The sightings were not restricted to Madison. Chronicles came in from the Pacific Ocean to the Atlantic Coast and across at least eighteen different states. Witnesses, as they do, seemed to see many different things. Some commonalities among reports were descriptions of a cigar-shaped object, a huge ball of fire or a large egg on its side. Other witnesses reported hearing voices emanating from the UFO and large beams of light reaching the ground. Many descriptions given by witnesses indicated that perhaps the object was an early dirigible—many descriptions, but not all. A number of narratives gave observations contradictory to the dirigible hypothesis, such as the object moving against the wind and at speeds of over one hundred miles per hour. I love how the papers of the time document the credibility of the witnesses as "Wisconsin Judges, good church going folk and those not predisposed to drink whisky." With that litany, my own credibility surely would have been called into question.

The *Madison Democrat* ran a front-page article titled "Airship Explained." The article reported that "railroad men" accused the Ringling Brothers of being the source of the great airship sightings. The airship was seen hovering "suspiciously long over the Winter Quarters at Baraboo" of those "RINGLING RAZZLEDAZZLERS."

In David Michael Jacob's book *The UFO Controversy in America*, he documented witness testimony from Milwaukee. He noted that possibly thousands of persons watched "the machine, or whatever it was," as it hovered over city hall. Even with more than one hundred years of research and investigation into this UFO wave, UFOlogists and historians alike are no closer to unraveling the mystery.

The lake monster mystery continued a few years later. This case showcases Wisconsinites' fortitude for survival. It was June 1897, and Eugene Heath, who was reported to be a machinery salesman, went at least one step beyond being a static witness. When he saw the serpent looking like an overturned boat and twice as long, he took two shots at it with his gun. The Lake Monona sighting was picked up by papers, which ran headlines like "Bullets Had No Effects on the Hide." In an apparent response, the serpent turned

The article in the upper right corner is titled "Airship Explained." *Image courtesy of the Madison Democrat,* Tuesday morning edition, April 13, 1897.

and rushed toward Heath. Wasting no time, our once brave witness quickly fled the area. Perhaps he had been so brazen with bullets because it was rumored throughout the city that, a week earlier, the serpent had eaten a local dog while it was swimming in Lake Monona. Perhaps Mr. Heath was seeking revenge for man's best friend.

Others witnessed the creature as well. The owner of Shott's boat rentals, John Shott, and his family had spent years living and working on the lakes of Madison. The papers of the time reported that the Shotts' stance on the "monster" was "whatever it may be…it is a reality and not a joke or a creature of their combined imaginations."

On August 4, 1899, Mrs. E. Grove and Mrs. J.J. Pecher found themselves drawn to the shoreline of Lake Mendota. They were in the area on a camping trip with several other women. They all became witnesses to what was later dubbed the "Lake Mendota Sea Serpent" by the *Racine Daily Journal.* The campers had decided to spend some time on the waters, enjoying the area from a boat. It was reported in the paper that the ladies described "a long, snake-like monster with a head ten inches across, and a tail which had horns." Frightened, the ladies hurried for shore as the serpent "plunged…into the depths of the lake, making a great deal of foam." Only eighteen days later, the serpent was seen again.

This time, Barney Reynolds was the witness. The sighting occurred on Lake Mendota again, this time near Bernard Boat Yard. About this same time, on nearby Lake Waubesa, the serpent also reared its ugly head—literally. That sighting is detailed in the Southern Madison chapter.

It is certainly no secret that hoaxes were frequently reported in the newspapers of the 1800s and earlier. This was a popular tradition and served to entertain readers for weeks on end as the stories continued to grow with each printing. The papers also used these fantastical and fictional stories as a way to increase readership through word-of-mouth buzz. It is, however, widely accepted that by the 1900s, these hoaxes were becoming more out of favor and were being replaced with objective journalism. While they are still found after 1900, traditionally they are overly dramatic and clearly not meant for news consumption.

Just to show that the mysteries of Madison can run from the mundane to the outright macabre, let's step into our next mystery from 1900. Showcasing the macabre for this entry is Miss Myrtle E. Downing and her shoes made from human skin. Indeed, the newspaper *Milwaukee Journal* pointedly titled the piece "Madison Girl Wears Shoes Made from Human Skin." The shoes were apparently a gift "sent to her by a Madison boy who is attending medical college in Chicago." The shoes were described as "tan in color with black toes and black stitching." The raw material for the shoes "was taken from the leg of an unknown man who was murdered in the streets of Chicago." Perhaps as only a mother could, the paper shared that Mrs. Downing "showed considerable pride in her daughter's shoes and said she knew of no reason why she should not wear them." Even the Presbyterian Church got involved, with one of its members remarking, "I do not see that there is any sin in it." Mrs. Downing spoke further on the matter, discussing the school in Chicago. "You know the first thing they do is to peel the body," she said, and then took it another step, adding, "Myrtle had a picture sent to her where the boys were peeling bodies." The paper noted that "Myrtle is a pretty girl, 18 years of age." It revealed in the end of the article that "Miss Downing received more than enough tanned human hide to make the pair of shoes." Perhaps you got from the earlier quotes that she made the shoes herself. If so, nice work, because I missed it! Maybe that's a 1900 version of a plot twist? The paper closed by noting that she was "thinking up" something else to make with what was left, suggesting "perhaps a pocket book."

Now, I've never been under the delusion that my own paranormal investigators' research organization was Madison's first. In fact, about the same time in the 1990s as I was putting together my formal group, Madison had two other organizations of people doing the same. The following story from 1905 proves without a doubt that passion for the paranormal has a long-rooted history in the area. Perhaps not a mystery itself, the Mediums' Protective Association did deal regularly with mysteries in and around the Madison area. The *Eau Claire Leader* ran a story titled "Spook Union Is Formed" detailing how "Wisconsin Mediums File Articles for a Protective Association." The paper reported that the association's aim was to "issue the mediums a working card, which will authorize them to interview spirits and receive and transmit messages." Of course, this was "so long as they live up to the rules of the association." At the printing of the article, the association already had fourteen members, twelve of whom were Madison residents. Apparently, the members felt the need for a moderating association due to "the number of 'fake' mediums."

Even though the capitol had burned down two years earlier, in 1906 the question on everyone's minds was whether the city was cursed. This mystery has less to do with monsters or mediums and more to do with mysteries of the mind. The *Eau Claire Leader* published the headline "Cursed City Still There," followed with "Preacher's Prophecy Fails and Scared Madison Folk Return." The scare came when "the prophecy of a religious exhorter… declared that the lakes would rise up and engulf the city." The prophet, who went by "Professor Jones," held meetings in the streets of Madison. One meeting grew so large that the professor was "arrested for obstructing traffic." It may have been this run-in with the law that gave rise to his allegedly cursing the city and making his fantastic flood prediction. The paper went on to report that "hundreds of persons last night left the city," presumably in fear of the ensuing floodwaters. The paper later went on to mention "sheepishly, quiet and shamefacedly, 1,500 residents of Madison came back to their homes last night after having spent twenty-four hours in waiting to hear that Madison had sunk."

I think the true mystery is why 1,500 Madison residents let themselves believe the word of one man with no empirical or quantitative data. Fifteen hundred people are a lot in my mind—even today, when the population is well over 200,000. Back then, the population was closer to 20,000. That's a fair chunk of the townsfolk who fled. The article went on to plainly share that "there was no disturbance here today." The people went to summer parks, baseball games and other amusement places as usual.

In September 1910, the airship was again sighted over Madison. This time, Lake Mendota was home to the sighting (sans serpents). A "ship" far above the water approached from the north. It was reported in the *Wisconsin State Journal* that it began slowing, "descending, hovering, as if seeking a place to land." The article, outlined in Jay Rath's *The W-Files*, documented the object, which it said then headed out of sight to the "southwest." If people were at the controls of these airships, it was never proven. As a result, these sightings are one of the great mysteries of the 1800s.

Crimes against children are easily beyond words. While life had many differences in 1911, there were also many similarities. Kidnapping and murder was unfortunately one of them. On the evening of September 5, or in the early morning of the sixth, second grader Annie Lemberger disappeared from her bed.

By most accounts, it was a typical evening in the Lemberger home. Their home was a small cottage located in the now historic Greenbush neighborhood of Madison, at 2 South Frances Street.

Not much of the original Frances Street remains in Madison today, 2011. *Photograph by Noah Voss.*

The parents had put their children to bed by seven o'clock. Mom and dad slept with their bedroom door ajar, as was common of the times. This helped keep the single heat source for the entire home flowing through, well, the entire home. The family dog did what it normally did after the rest of the family was asleep. Annie shared a small room with her sister and two brothers. The bedroom where all four children slept was reportedly only eight feet by eight feet in size. Marv Balousek, in his book *101 Wisconsin Unsolved Mysteries*, documented that the other children asleep in the room "hadn't heard a thing." Mrs. Lemberger "had locked all the doors and the window, including the one above Annie's bed."

Mr. Lemberger walked police through his suspicions of how the perpetrator must have kidnapped Annie: "Someone must have torn the mosquito netting on the outside, then removed a piece of cracked glass from the window above Annie's bed and reached inside to open it." Author Marv Balousek continued reporting the father's theory: "Then the culprit must have propped up the window with a piece of lath and quietly grabbed Annie from her bed and through the window." The police reported footprints outside the window; however, the crowd of angry residents pushing to get a glimpse of the crime scene trampled the prints. Everyone was a suspect.

The gypsy camp just south of Madison was searched by authorities, as was every empty building, sewer system and train car. There was even talk of a door-to-door search to be conducted by angry mobs of Madison residents. A bloodhound was brought in and given Annie's clothing to acquire her scent. The bloodhound followed the same trail several times. It was one that cut through five blocks right to Lake Monona. On September 7, the mayor shared through the *Wisconsin State Journal* that he was offering a "Reward for Recovery" of $200. It was conveyed in some corners that Mr. Martin Lemberger had consulted a "spiritualist," who divined that Annie was taken away in a covered wagon and was being held captive west of Madison. Still, there was no sign of Annie.

A new suspect was found in neighbor John A. Johnson. John had previously been convicted of "damaging a train" and assaulting "three young girls," according to author Marv Balousek. John's past also included two separate admissions to Mendota Mental Health Institute in Madison. Those two stays in Mendota were the result of "assaulting a young girl" and "the attempted sexual assault of two young girls ages seven and ten." As far as suspects go, John was at the top of the list and was questioned but released early on. The Lemberger family was too poor to be a target for ransom, so the crime's motivation seemed clear. There was one major problem with the prime suspect, however: his alibi.

John had a shaky alibi, which was corroborated by three family members. His wife and two daughters told police that they were home when John arrived at about 9:00 p.m. Their home was just down the block from the Lembergers' home. Annie was put to bed at about 7:00 p.m. that same evening, leaving a small but manageable window of opportunity for Mr. Johnson to visit the Lembergers' house.

Then a body was found.

George Younger ran into the local saloon owned by Bruno Kleinheinz looking for help in retrieving something he had seen floating in Brittingham Bay on Lake Monona. The crew that followed found the lifeless, nude body of Annie Lemberger.

An autopsy was performed and found that Annie's lungs held no water, indicating she was dead by the time she was left in the water. There were bruises found on the left side of her head, above her eye and behind her ear. Gossip suggested that there might have been other details discovered during her autopsy that were kept quiet for decency's sake.

Brittingham Bay today is a popular park just off East Washington Avenue and Park Streets, 2011. *Photograph by Noah Voss.*

John was again taken into custody. This time, thanks to $10,000 raised by the *Wisconsin State Journal*, Detective Edward L. Boyer was on the scene. Boyer was a well-known detective out of Chicago who worked for the respected William Burns Detective Agency.

On September 9, the *Wisconsin State Journal* expressed the general mood of Madisonians in an editorial: "The dirtiest and most damnable kind of murder has been committed here. So long as this murderer is at large and so long as a murder of this kind can be committed with impunity, no child in Madison is safe."

Detective Boyer questioned John, and reportedly, when asked specifically where the nightgown was that Annie had been wearing the night of her disappearance, he replied, "I can't tell." Those investigating the case took this as a partial confession of John's guilt. Detective Boyer warned John not to venture close to the windows in his cell, as the mob outside was preparing to lynch him. Perhaps the detective was trying to impress on him the direness of his situation, or maybe he simply wanted John to face legal punishment for his crime before his death. It was recounted by some that Detective Boyer was investigating leads of boys kidnapping Annie, as he felt the broken windowpane was too small for an adult hand to reach through. Soon, the detective was not going to need any other leads.

On September 25, 1911, John Johnson confessed to the murderous crimes against Annie Lemberger. In newspapers as far away as the *New York Times*, it was reported, "In the presence of the Chief of Police, the District Attorney, and Foye, Johnson described how he had taken the girl from her bedroom, through the open window, which he had forced open." He took her to the railroad bridge, he said, beat her to death and then threw the body into the lake. Since he pleaded guilty to the crime of murder, there was no trial, and he was sent to Waupun State Prison for a sentence of life. That could have been the end of the story, mystery solved.

It was not the end, but the beginning of yet another twist in this murder mystery.

No sooner had he arrived in Waupun than John Johnson stated, "Well, the mob didn't get me, and I didn't kill Annie Lemberger." These declarations of innocence continued for another ten years, until our next twist.

In the fall of 1921, after swearing his innocence to anyone who would listen, John was able to convince Governor John Blaine to hold an appeals hearing with the help of his new attorney, Ole A. Stolen.

Judge Hoppmann oversaw the hearing for John's pardon application. From the start, it seemed John's case was based on recanting his original confession that he had indeed kidnapped and killed Annie Lemberger. John stated he had given that confession to avoid mob justice at the end of a rope. To counter this, the prosecutors were able to produce several police officers who swore under oath that John was not coerced in any way during his original confession. As difficult as it must have been, the Lemberger family was present to show strength and solidarity against the convicted killer of their child. They were surely anticipating watching the murderer be sent back to prison for life. However, the case took on a disturbing turn after the weekend recess.

Ole A. Stolen represented John Johnson, and on Monday morning, he introduced new evidence. Mr. Stolen addressed the packed courtroom, "Now I am prepared to prove who killed Annie Lemberger. Annie Lemberger came to her death by blows struck by her own father! Sheriff, serve your warrants." The courtroom must have reacted loudly. The Lembergers must have been beyond dumbfounded.

Mrs. Sorenson, the key witness, took the stand. A family friend, Mrs. Sorenson testified that she had stopped by the Lembergers' home soon after hearing about the disappearance of Annie. She spoke about "finding blood spots on the sheets and pillow slip of the bed in which Annie had lain." Mrs. Sorenson went on to say that she knew Mrs. Lemberger had burned Annie's bloodstained nightgown in the kitchen stove. In a dramatic turn, Mrs. Sorenson shared that Mrs. Lemberger had a "fainting spell" during that same visit. Upon awaking, Mrs. Lemberger cried out, "Martin, Martin, why did you do it?" according to Sorenson.

Mrs. Sorenson again visited the Lemberger home after Annie's funeral. She shared with the courtroom that while comforting the oldest Lemberger boy, Alois, he confided in her the details of the night Annie disappeared. In the *Capital Times*, she was reported as saying that the Lembergers "had a beer and whiskey party at the house the night before and that Annie, who had gone to bed, got up for a drink." Her father demanded a poker (for the fire), but Annie failed to find it, whereupon her father struck her. After hitting Annie in the head with a beer bottle, Annie fell on the stove and was then placed in her bed, unconscious. After discovering she had died, "the father took the body to the cellar, hiding it in a tub." The father "hired" a man "by the name of Davis to carry the body to the lake." Mrs. Sorenson spoke in court about how Mr. Lemberger had threatened to "choke her" if she spoke of the matter and how Mrs. Lemberger begged her not to disgrace the family name.

The family was again forced to take the stand, but this time in defense of their own innocence. By the end of that day, three of the Lembergers were charged and arrested. Mr. Martin Lemberger was charged with manslaughter. Mrs. Magdalene Lemberger and the oldest son, Alois, were charged with perjury.

The pardon hearing for John Johnson was postponed until the outcome of the trial for the Lemberger family could be determined. John was placed back in jail to wait. The three Lembergers were also placed in jail until their trial. District Attorney Lewis asked "that he be relieved as prosecutor of the Lembergers because of his confidential relations with them during the Johnson hearing and his belief that they were innocent." Mr. Martin Lemberger didn't go to trial until January of the following year. On January 5, 1922, Mr. Lemberger's lawyers successfully argued that the statute of limitations for the crime had run out. Judge Hoppman dismissed the charges, and Mr. Martin Lemberger was released from custody the same day. John Johnson was eventually released from prison, having his sentence commuted on February 17, 1922. John Johnson died years later, supposedly due to "drinking." He is interred at Forest Hill Cemetery in Section 25. One final twist was to come.

In 1933, the Lemberger family and Mrs. Sorenson were put to a polygraph, or lie detector, test. The accuracy of polygraph tests in actually determining whole and often complicated truths is widely debatable, even today with the advances of nearly a century. In 1933, they epitomized the mysticism of science, and the Lemberger family all passed, proclaiming their innocence. Then it was Mrs. Sorenson's turn, and her story read false. When confronted with this information, she confessed to taking $500 to lie in her testimony against the Lembergers during their trial. The person who had approached and bribed her was none other than John Johnson's attorney. Unfortunately, no new information was forthcoming providing a decisively clear killer of Annie Lemberger. She eventually found her way to Resurrection Cemetery on Madison's west side. She is still there today, laid to rest as Anna Lemberger. Her marker in Section H-6 includes a birth date, a kidnapped date and the final day death found her.

In 1917, on Lake Mendota, a man fishing along the shore around a still popular area called Picnic Point watched something emerge from the water less than one hundred feet away. What he witnessed was so mysterious that he ran from the area, leaving behind all his equipment. *The W-Files* recorded that the man witnessed "a large snake-like head, with large jaws and blazing eyes." The author, Mr. Rath, goes on to share that the witness and "his story were ridiculed."

By this time, the creature sightings had taken on a name in most circles; it was called "Bozho." The name for the local lake monster came from area natives, who had stories of their own godlike creature, Winnebozho or

Lake Mendota, as viewed from Bascom Hill. Picnic Point is on the left, 2011. *Photograph by Noah Voss.*

Nanabozho. This deity makes an appearance in most all indigenous peoples' oral traditions. Many times, Bozho is portrayed as a shape-shifter, trickster or even skinwalker. For those wanting to learn more and needing to stay up at night, I would highly recommend George Knapp and Colm A. Kelleher's *Hunt for the Skinwalker* nonfiction book.

Many of the experiences found in *Mysterious Madison* can be traced back to Wisconsin's best-known historian, Charles E. Brown. He was the first in many regards, founding many of the historical societies that are still around in one form or another today. Any published works showcasing unexplained history from Wisconsin that date to before the 1950s very likely passed by Mr. Brown's ears and eventually his pen. The legends and lore that Mr. Brown documented at times were saved from the eventual obscurity that befalls many oral traditions. One such story came from Mrs. Anna White Wings. Mr. Brown documented her experience with what is now the area called Picnic Point. She claimed that witches once skulked through the darkened underbrush. They sought small children to fatten up for only they knew what purpose, though Mrs. Wings speculated that the kids were eaten by the witches. It was her belief that the "Earthmaker" punished the witches and stopped the carnage. By capturing the witches and then turning them into hackberry trees, the Earthmaker forced upon them the pain of feeding the children without the power of eating them after.

Police officer Grant Dosch worked the Schenk's Corners area in what was Eastern Madison in 1918. Returning home from his third-shift patrol on February 4, he was driving down West Washington Avenue. Author Marv Balousek, in his book *101 Wisconsin Unsolved Mysteries*, records that Officer Dosch "noticed something suspicious going on" at a general merchandise store. According to a *Capital Times* article written a few years after the incident, the store was at 741 West Washington Avenue. Thirty-year-old Officer Dosch approached the general store owned by Louis Cohen, pulling off his gloves and out his gun. A shot thundered through the crisp winter air. Officer Dosch's revolver had not fired, but another assailant, who was hiding across the street, had unloaded both barrels of his shotgun into Officer Dosch. Dosch was not killed instantly, despite having been hit in the head by both shots. The burglars fled the scene, where Officer Dosch was found soon after by nearby resident Elmer Currie. Mr. Currie was awakened, not by the shotgun blast, but by the painful moaning of the officer. Officer Dosch was taken to St. Mary's Hospital, where he was treated by Dr. Joseph Dean. The officer never regained consciousness. Officer Dosch succumbed to his wounds seven hours later, leaving behind a wife and two kids.

Eight officers were assigned to the case, tasked to find the murderers

Saturday 10th Anniversary of Murder of Patrolman; Still Mystery

Dosch First of 3 Officers to be Slain

3 Men Held for Crime Acquitted After Sensa-

Died At Hospital

Mr. Currie found Officer Dosch unconscious on the sidewalk, his fully loaded gun lying at his side and his cap and gloves lying in the snow a short distance away.

The wounded officer was taken to a local hospital, where he succumbed to severe several hours later.

Police started an investigation and secured as an assistant an Italian detective attached to the Beloit police force.

With the discovery that the Louis Cohen general merchandise store, 754 W. Washington ave., had been robbed, police worked under the theory that

The men were not brought to trial until more than a year after they had been placed under arrest. They were held in the county jail during the entire period.

Men Are Acquitted

The trial was started on Apr. 7, 1919, and eleven days later the jury returned the not guilty verdict, and the men were released from custody.

Since the killing of Dosch, two other Madison policemen have been murdered in the "Bush."

In December, 1924, Patrolman Herbert Dreger was shot in the first block on S. Murray st. Two Sicilians were

A decade after the murder of Officer Dosch, the community was still following the mystery. *Image courtesy of the* Capital Times, *February 1, 1928.*

of Officer Dosch. In an article in the *Capital Times*, police "secured as an assistant an Italian detective attached to the Beloit police force." The same paper ran an article ten years after the murder outlining the case, including the trial. A wagon full of stolen goods from the general merchandise store was discovered on the same block as the crime. It was found in a vacant barn. The only clue left at the scene of the crime was the shotgun used to kill Officer Dosch. It had been reloaded after the initial two shots and reportedly "led police to believe that the killing was the work of Sicilians." The police questioned forty people, with "the probe leading to the arrest of…four men." The fourth arrested "Sicilian, Frank Mazzaro, was committed to the state hospital at Mendota, before the trial."

A trial finally came on April 7, 1919. Even though it took more than a year, the three suspects had spent the "entire period" in the county jail. Eleven days later, "the jury returned the not guilty verdict and the men were released from custody." John and Tony Mazzaro, along with Peter Mcsena, were free men once again.

Very likely, the decision by the killers, whoever they were, to leave all the stolen property behind allowed their identities to remain a mystery to this day. Perhaps it was the thieves' original plan to return for the loot, before they became murderers.

A modern street sign, not far from where the killers would have hidden their loot, 2011. *Photograph by Noah Voss.*

Central Madison

The Greenbush area of Madison in the 1920s was referred to as "Little Italy" by residents throughout the county. The locals of Little Italy had their own nicknames for parts of their neighborhood, like Death's Corner. Who knew Madison had a Death's Corner? The intersection of Murray Street and Desmond Court in the 1920s was well known as such. Sadly, this area can no longer be found using the street names. Many roadways have been renamed or removed completely since the 1920s, as new city plans became more desirable than old streets. The area earned its intriguing title due to several attacks and murders that happened in the immediate vicinity. Here are just a few of the more mysterious cases.

In August 1922, James D'Amico sat on a small ledge in the front of his store at 16 South Murray Street. He was chatting away the evening with Arnao, co-owner of the grocery. At 9:00 p.m., Arnao reported that a loud bang and crack rang out. The thunderous explosion of a double-barreled shotgun discharging into the back of his business partner, paired with the crashing of the business's window, shattered the once pleasant autumn eve.

What many Madisonians may not have known before this fateful night is that James D'Amico was a "connected" man. It was suspected that James D'Amico had made his money as a mob figure in Chicago, going by the name Jimmy D'Amico. He had emigrated from a small city in Sicily at the age of twenty-five. His connections may have been the reason he disappeared from Chicago one day with his wife and child. Though many people searched for him, it simply became accepted that he was no longer around. He had indeed secretly relocated to Madison, Wisconsin.

James's brother, Angelo D'Amico, had only recently died in much the same way in Chicago. James D'Amico had returned to Chicago for the funeral a month earlier and in doing so may have tipped off his future killers to his whereabouts. James may have very well known that his brother's gangland end was foretelling. Those questioned after the shooting in Madison shared that James was "nervous throughout the day and had complained of being sick."

Police back in Madison arrived at the gruesome scene of James D'Amico's body riddled with four slugs, strewn about his storefront. Arnao told police that James cried out, "Oh My God!" and toppled over on the floor dead. Further investigation by police and investigative reporters for the *Capital Times* discovered three additional .32-caliber rounds lodged in the back of the store. Two shooters were present during the killing of James D'Amico. Newspapers jumped at the chance to report this murder mystery with colorful introductions to their articles such as the following one from the *Capital Times*: "Plunging into the labyrinth of gang intrigue, which has reached its highest stage of development among Italian residents of American cities, winding its tentacles about the wealthy and the penniless of that nationality, Madison police investigated the murder of James D'Amico." The papers even called into question Arnao's seating choice. It was speculated that perhaps Arnao knew of the impending hit on James and chose to sit awkwardly out of the way, at a distance from the front of the store. This Madison murder mystery remains unsolved to this day. However, Madison, Wisconsin, and the mob would not part ways for good.

But life has smaller things to offer. For instance, the smallest doll in the world! This was claimed to be in Madison not once, but twice. On October 1, 1922, the *Wisconsin State Journal* ran an article titled "Smallest Doll in the World Is Owned by Engineer Student." The doll was "dressed and jointed." It stood less than one inch tall and was the property of Frederick Gustave, who had moved from Chicago to attend the University of Madison. Mr. Gustave didn't make the doll but rather related that "it has been in his mother's family for so many generations that they forgot to keep count of them." The construction was wood and more precisely was "seven-eighths of an inch high." The capitol building had recently burned, and it was noted in the same article that the museum on-site had also displayed an item labeled "the smallest doll in the world." That doll sadly perished in the fire but stood a full half inch taller than Gustave's doll. Charles Brown, curator of the Wisconsin State Historical Museum was consulted and "declared that it is one of the finest pieces of workmanship he has ever seen."

Dolls aside, world's smallest or no, within six months the murderous mob connections were again playing out in the papers. The motive put forth by police on Wednesday, February 14, 1923, for "the mysterious slaying of Joseph Justo, 38, father of the convict, who was found dying in the snow on Murray St.," was vengeance. The police arrived at this conclusion due to Justo's son's involvement in one of the more egregious offenses to the mob: he squealed. While any official connection of the Justo family to the mob was never established, their own family of four was certainly organized in crime. Mr. Justo's son Dominic was serving a "five-year term in Waupun for complicity in the robbery of the Randall State Bank." It is believed the conviction of another in the same robbery was only possible because Dominic implicated fellow bank robber Corona. The Justo family had an illustrious history with Madison Police. Mr. Justo's youngest son, age fifteen, was in "Waukesha Industrial School serving a sentence for highway robbery." Other past offenses on the Justo's family record were for both Mr. and Mrs. Justo, who had been found guilty of violating the "state dry law, after they

A sign for Milton Street, of which little remains from the 1920s. *Photograph by Noah Voss.*

had been found guilty in federal court." They were again arrested only the week before Justo's murder when police "found six quarts of moonshine hidden in a piano bench at his home 810 Milton St."

Mr. Justo's end was reported with dirty detail in the *Capital Times*: "The assassin creeping upon Justo as he was walking along Murray St., must have placed the gun almost at the base of his head, then pulled the trigger." The police were not able to find any witnesses who would say they heard a thing, even though someone had unloaded a shotgun in the middle of the sidewalk at 6:30 p.m. The police said that Mr. Justo was likely "the member of one of the two factions warring for supremacy in the foreign section."

December 1924 saw the youngest police officer on the Madison force killed. Officer Herbert Dreger was found by John Dempsey as he lay in the street bleeding profusely. Captain Harry Davenport was night commander on the evening of the shooting. He deployed to Death's Corner and was the first of the police to reach Officer Dreger. Officer Dreger was bundled in blankets, placed in the back of a police car and taken to the hospital. He managed to speak only briefly. "Those guys in the—" His words trailed off,

A shotgun similar to those used often in the gang-ridden streets of 1920s Madison. *Photograph by Noah Voss.*

and as he regained strength, he continued, "—got me." He survived for less than one hour. His wife arrived at his side, holding Herbert in her arms as his life slipped away.

Officer Dreger's "post mortem revealed that 59 slugs from a shotgun had entered" his body. Whoever the attacker was, he took extra effort to make sure the officer would not recover, as "a revolver bullet hole through his neck" was later found. The *Waukesha Daily Freeman* reported that the shot to the neck "indicated that the slayer(s) wanted to make sure the policeman would not be able to talk." Talk he was just barely able to do. It was stated that he was able to give his fellow officers enough information to make several arrests.

Part of the shotgun suspected to have been used to shoot the officer was left at the scene of the crime. The other half was found within days on a prime suspect by the name of "Sam" Di Martino. He also happened to have been arrested by Officer Dreger three weeks earlier on a "charge of driving an automobile while intoxicated, and was convicted and fined." Frank Vitale and Salvatore Di Martino were both put on trial but acquitted by a Sauk County circuit court jury. It would be a long holiday season for

Officer Dreger's wife, who waited through two months of trials only to have a not guilty verdict. As far as the courts are concerned, the murder of Officer Herbert Dreger remains a mystery. The chief suspect who stood trial for the murder, Sam Di Martino, died a free man, of natural causes, in 1927.

In the news reports following the slaying of Officer Dreger, it would seem that he knew the risks of Greenbush. He had spoken with his brother only the week before about his fears. "I'm afraid one of those fellows will shoot a little too fast for me someday," he said. Sergeant Clarence Bullard expressed his feelings for Officer Dreger: "He was the most cool-headed man on the force." To add to the mystery, or perhaps offer a potential cause for Officer Dreger's murder, the Ku Klux Klan showed up in force at the funeral. In the spirit of full disclosure, I will quickly state that I was unable to find out whether Officer Dreger was a member of the Klan or its members simply showed up due to their support of police agencies around the country at the time. The Ku Klux Klan, or KKK, was born out of the Confederate army in the mid-1860s. Initially a terrorist organization bent on changing the government with violent insurgency tactics, by the 1920s the Klan had evolved into an organization outspoken in its support of racism, anti-Catholicism, anti-Semitism and anti-Communism. The neighborhood that Officer Dreger had been patrolling on the night of his murder was widely known as Madison's "mixing pot" of heritage. The KKK's tactics were regularly violent, and at the time of Officer Dreger's murder, its membership may have numbered

The funeral for Officer Dreger was attended by more people than the church could accommodate. *WHS-35726.*

as high as five million throughout the United States. Another reason known Klan members would not have been welcomed in Greenbush was their growing support for temperance and the Prohibition movement. Greenbush had a lucrative network of bootleggers hawking booze for hefty profits.

Death's Corner strikes again! A man by the name of Julius Ucello was wounded in thirteen places in an attack on January 12, 1924, with a sawed-off shotgun. He physically recovered from the attack.

The *Capital Times* ran a story in March 1924 that outlined "Little Italy's rum war, which Sunday night claimed its fourth victim, Anton Navarra, grocer, alleged leader of one of two warring factions in the foreign settlement on the West Side…a feud between two groups of Italian bootleggers, each of which speaks a distinct dialect and each of which occupies a separate street." Mr. Navarra had just stepped behind his grocery counter when an unidentified assailant on the street lifted his double-barreled shotgun and pulled the trigger. The front window shattered as bullets crashed through the glass and into Mr. Navarra. The paper reported that "Navarra reeled and started for the ante room, but fell on the steps." He could go no farther, "nine slugs" having ripped through his body. The triggerman was said by one witness to have dashed away from the window, down the "side of the building, hurtled a fence at the rear of the store and after throwing away his weapon on an ash pile, made his get-away through shadows on Milton St."

Mr. Navarra, at the age of thirty-eight, became the third Italian slain in a similar manner in the last eighteen months. The *Capital Times* went on to explain, "Natural enemies because of the age-old feuds waged between their forefathers in Italy, the warfare here has broken out afresh in recent months because of disputes over moonshine price cutting." The reporter continued that Mr. Navarra was the believed leader of the Regent Street Clan and that "both clans, each of which had been prospering in the moonshine traffic, began reducing liquor prices in order to drive the other faction out of business." This back-and-forth price war quickly escalated into street violence and repeated murder at the end of a double-barreled shotgun.

Lewis Lotwin was shot in four places and left for dead by someone police thought held a "grudge" against him. In 1924, Mr. Lotwin was headed to work as a "barn man" on the morning he was attacked. The papers of the time reported that "as he passed death corner…his assailant darted from behind a garage in the rear of a grocery store and fired into Lotwin's back." Interestingly, Mr. Lotwin was actually wealthy enough to retire and had even recently donated $1,000 to a local hospital. He was thought by most to be a bit of a recluse, had never married and died without identifying his killer.

"When a murderer's gun boomed in Madison's Bush Monday night, another woman became a widow." That was the caption printed under Mrs. Di Martino's photograph when it appeared in the *Capital Times* on April 10, 1928. Joe Di Martino was visiting friends at 22 South Murray Street. He and four other people, including one eleven-year-old, talked in the kitchen. Mr. Di Martino rose from his chair in preparation of departing. Little did he know that in the rear of the house, crouching in the shadows, was a killer taking aim. As Mr. Di Martino stood, the killer "pulled both triggers of the full length, double-barrelled [*sic*], 12-gauge shotgun." It was said that "when the heavy buckshot from both barrels of the gun struck him, Di Martino plunged across the kitchen and through the door leading into the dining room." He fell as he crossed the threshold into the dining room, his head striking against an axe lying on the floor. The assassin was never caught. Mr. Di Martino sustained "seventeen wounds...found in his body when examined at the Schroeder funeral home." Fifteen slugs had entered his chest and two

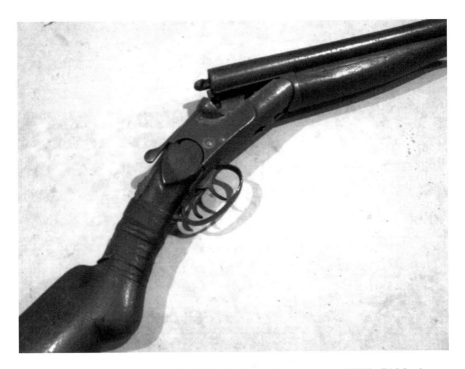

A double-barreled shotgun from the 1920s, similar to the one used to kill Mr. Di Martino. *Photograph by Noah Voss.*

penetrated his left arm. The paper reported gruesome details, including that six slug pellets were "found to have gone through the body and to have lodged under the skin of the back." The first police to arrive on the scene found Mr. Di Martino to have a pulse for only a few moments.

The shotgun used in the killing was found where it was believed to have been dropped, about fifteen feet outside the window. Mr. Di Martino also held the distinction of being the "15th to be murdered in Sicilian Colony" in less than fifteen years. Those with murder in their hearts were busy around Death's Corner in Madison. The regular trouble from that area allowed the papers to simply refer to it as "the fateful corner." People would just know which corner they were referring to.

Happily moving into lighter fare, we arrive at October 1938. This tale has many mysterious angles but is not quite so murderous; however, with genocidal aliens aimed at annihilating the human race, things could get dark. Thankfully for us, it was only a fictional radio show, though many at the time were unaware of its fictional status. For the Halloween season, Wisconsin-born Orson Welles took his national radio listenership through a radio theater program. It was titled *War of the Worlds*, by H.G. Wells, and was based on a science fiction book from 1898.

MERCURY THEATER

The role of the narrator, who is one of the few humans to survive the invasion of Earth by inhabitants of Mars, will be filled by Orson Welles when the Mercury Theater broadcasts an adaptation of H. G. Wells' "War of the Worlds," tonight on WBBM at 7 o'clock.

SUNDAY HOUR

A newspaper clipping of the Mercury Theater listing for the evening's radio shows. *Image courtesy of the* Capital Times, *Sunday morning edition, October 30, 1938.*

The aftermath, as shown in this front-page title: "'Attack From Mars' on Radio Program Brings Near-Panic to Nation." *Image courtesy of the* Capital Times, *Monday, October 31, 1938.*

The advertisement run in the newspaper clearly stated, "The role of the narrator, who is of the few humans to survive the invasion of Earth by inhabitants of Mars, will be filled by Orson Welles." It went on to share that the program was "an adaptation of H.G. Wells' 'War of the Worlds,' tonight on WBBM at 7 o'clock."

If you've never had the pleasure of listening to a recording or rebroadcast of the original Mercury Theater program of *War of the Worlds*, let me tell you, it is a treat. The AM monotone sound on an often dirty recording, full of scratches and dust, makes for a romantic listen on a crisp October evening. The program starts innocently enough, stating similar information as the newspaper ad, but after only several moments, the host comes back on, seemingly interrupting the program with breaking narratives of "explosions" visible on Mars. The act is not broken until the end, and much happens before that. The Crosby Service estimated that over thirty-two million people were listening to the program that night. The *New York Times* famously reported on its front page the next day that "Radio Listeners in Panic, Taking War Drama as Fact." The article went on to state that "many flee homes to escape gas raid from Mars—phone calls swamp police."

The response to the radio program in Madison was tame compared to some other parts of the country, where "apartment houses in New York were emptied hurriedly by frantic listeners…newspaper offices and police stations everywhere were swamped with calls from terrified people, many of them weeping…woman in Pittsburgh tried suicide, saying 'I'd rather die this way than like that.'"

The *Capital Times* article goes on to say that local Madison "radio station WIBA received about 20 telephone inquiries." Interestingly, most of the callers were "indignant" because they were scared about what was happening with the alien invaders and quite annoyed that WIBA was not broadcasting the events. The article went on to state that "most of the inquiries were from women." At press, the *Capital Times* reported that the Madison Police and Sheriff's Department "had received no calls and knew nothing about the

'Invasion From Mars' Fails to Cause Big Flurry in City

MADISON residents are either too wise or too loyal to Charlie McCarthy to be excited by invasions from Mars.

That seemed the logical conclusion today after a search for any signs of alarm such as those that struck other communities from coast to coast following Orson Welles' broadcast of a radio sketch depicting such an invasion.

Welles, himself a former Madison youth, thought the skit "a bit old-fashioned." Madison listeners to his program did not have that reaction, but the only ...ness noticed here were those of curiosity.

Radio station WIBA received about 20 telephone inquiries, but almost all of the callers were a bit indignant because the local station carried no news broadcasts of the eastern "catastrophe." They felt WIBA was neglecting its listeners. Most of the inquiries were from women.

One man, however, apparently believed the radio playlet was a true news broadcast. Al Gilbert, WIBA announcer who received the telephone calls, said one man said he was "interested because he had relatives out that way."

Madison police and the sheriff's office, however, said they had received no calls and knew nothing about the broadcast.

This title reads, "'Invasion from Mars' Fails to Cause Big Flurry in City," referring to Madison, Wisconsin. *Image courtesy of the* Capital Times, *Monday afternoon edition, October 31, 1938.*

broadcast." Many Madison residents may have simply not tuned in. The very popular Charlie McCarthy had his own radio program, which ran at the same time that evening and very likely held many local listeners.

On the national stage, there was much attention given to Orson Welles's broadcast. The station that aired the program, CBS, the FCC and several American senators all took the opportunity to make attempts at strengthening their regulations of free speech.

Less than ten years later, the United States government would secretly but officially begin investigations into the UFO phenomenon, investigations that many claim are still operational to this day.

Project Blue Book may sound familiar to many people, especially those interested in unidentified flying objects. For everyone else, Project Blue Book was the first open investigation into the UFO phenomenon by America's federal government. More specifically, the United States Air Force, working in conjunction with private and enlisted specialists, was tasked to investigate the testimonies. How it got that far is often less discussed than the predetermined answers the air force was directed to discover.

An unclassified cover letter from Project Sign, titled "Unidentified Aerial Objects" and dated February 1949. *Image courtesy of the United States federal government.*

UFO historian Wendy Connors discovered some layered history in an interview with a former employee who worked as a secretary for Project Sign. In that interview, Connors discovered that the original name was "Project Saucer," and the investigations began in late 1946. This is new because for decades it was believed that Project Sign began after the Kenneth Arnold saucer sighting around Mount Saint Helens in 1947. These "projects" eventually evolved into Project Blue Book in 1949. Project Sign's directive was to "collect, collate, evaluate and distribute to interested government agencies and contractors all information concerning sightings and phenomena in the atmosphere which can be construed to be of concern to the national security."

Project Sign was an official United States government study instigated by Lieutenant General Nathan F. Twining. While head of the Air Materiel Command, Twining made the recommendation to those up the chain of command for such an operation. He may have been influenced by Brigadier General George Schulgen of the Army Air Forces Air Intelligence Division.

The brigadier general himself had just completed his own study of many UFO reports. His conclusion was that UFOs were real crafts. Brigadier General Schulgen had Lieutenant General Twining follow up his study with a more in-depth investigation into the phenomenon. This study was named Project Sign and was headquartered out of Wright-Patterson Air Force Base beginning in 1947. The project, categorized 2A priority, was one step away from the highest project ranking the United States Air Force could give.

Dr. Allen Hynek was consulted due to his professorship of astronomy at Ohio State University. He openly shared later in life that "I was quite

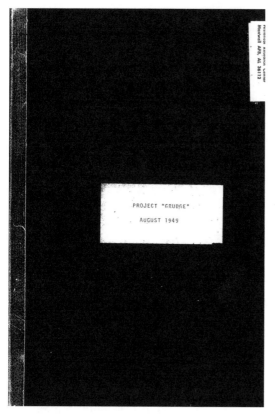

PROJECT "GRUDGE"
AUGUST 1949

Scan of the original unclassified Project Grudge black notebook, dated August 1949. *Image courtesy of the United States federal government.*

negative in most of my evaluations. I stretched far to give something a natural explanation, sometimes when it may not have really had it." Professor Hynek would go on to found his own UFO studies organization that would visit Madison in 1978 following a mysterious UFO encounter. The top scientists from around the country composed Project Sign. Though there was some division among its ranks, the team outlined in its reports how close it was to compiling enough data to prove its new leanings: UFOs were of extraterrestrial origin. You can read this for yourself in the unclassified report titled "Estimate of the Situation." Shortly after this new development, Project Sign was closed. It was replaced with Project Grudge and headed by several military personnel who had open and strong biases against UFOs. Their stance was that UFOs were not anything more than misidentifications made by "crackpots."

Under Project Grudge, everything was minimized, including staff, budgets and—arguably—interest in the truth. As the nonobjective stance of the people directing this new project was made known to higher-ups, the project was terminated. A new project, by the name of Project Blue Book, was born in 1952. Some of the best scientists were brought back from Project Sign. They worked diligently at solving a huge mystery for the world. However, Project Blue Book's directive had clearly changed by 1953. Though not officially ended until 1970, from 1953 on it is widely documented that Project Blue Book was used as an anti-UFO propaganda and misinformation tool.

It lived for only one year in true aspiration of objective science, seeking answers for only one year by most researchers' standards.

Indeed, to this day, what your neighbor thinks about the UFO phenomenon has been purposefully constructed by decades of propaganda to varying degrees emanating from Project Blue Book post 1953.

In Madison in 1952, a group of UFOs was again witnessed. This sighting, occurring only seven days after a formation of four UFOs, was followed for ten minutes by two pilots in their T-33s. On April 16, Mr. Dino of Lake Street in Madison watched with a friend while "5 or 6 objects in the sky" almost directly overhead defied identification. He was so perplexed by the sighting that he called the 176th Fighter Squadron Operations stationed at the Truax Air Field in Madison. It is documented in Project Blue Book that Operations contacted Captain R. Cambell at the radar station. Unfortunately, the radar was "off temporarily due to preventative maintenance; however, the sighting a week earlier had been scanned by operating radar, and the UFOs had no return on the radar scope. As stated in the Project Blue Book records, this sighting wasn't "outstanding," but because of the "excellent attempts" in identifying the objects by the ADC "the experience warranted further scrutiny." The ADC, or Air Defense Command, had the radar functioning within three minutes to help in identifying the objects. The radar scope showed no unknown returns.

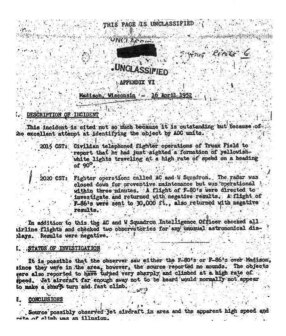

A redacted and cropped portion of an official Project Blue Book document giving a chronological synopsis of reported events during the April 16, 1952 Madison sighting. *Image courtesy of the United States federal government.*

An unclassified and redacted Project Blue Book document showing, in part III, the "Conclusions" of the investigation into the April 16, 1952 Madison sighting. *Image courtesy of the United States federal government.*

Mr. Dino and his friend were able to give a thorough description of the UFOs, stating for the record that they were "semi-circular in shape and formation… glowing with a yellowish-white light." He also added for investigators that there was no "sound nor exhaust" noted at the time of the sighting.

It was about 8:15 p.m. when the pair of friends watched as "the object(s) made a sharp turn in a North NW direction and gained altitude rapidly." As the UFOs rose, they "seemed to fuse or come together" and disappeared into the distance. By this time, Captain Cambell at Truax Air Field had redirected "some F-80-type" interceptor jet aircraft. The captain wanted to identify these UFOs, but unfortunately, scrambling the F-80s had "no results." Captain Cambell was not done; he "then took a flight of F-86 type aircraft at 30,000 ft over the area" and reported back sighting "nothing." He probably should have witnessed something if there were anything still around to see, as the weather was "clear and better than 15 miles visibility." Local commercial airlines were contacted and found to have no "flights in the vicinity" of the UFO sighting. Whatever it was the two friends had witnessed was at the very least not scheduled to be there. Even the two area astronomical observatories were contacted, including the University of Madison. Both observatories related back that "there was nothing unusual recorded."

In 1968, on the University of Wisconsin–Madison campus, Phillip Van Valkenberg was hurrying through the rain. He didn't have keys with him to Sterling Hall but thought he would knock on a friend's window to be let inside. As he pushed through some bushes to get to the side of the building, he stumbled upon the lifeless body of Christine Rothschild. When police arrived, they discovered that eighteen-year-old Christine "had been dead well over four hours." The *Capital Times* article recounted the tragedy in detail: "The cause of death was a puncture wound, one of 14 inflicted on the girl, which pierced her heart." The autopsy had also revealed "four broken ribs, caused by the puncture instrument, and a broken jaw which authorities believe resulted from a hard blow by a fist on the point of the chin." It was later reported that both her upper and lower jaws were broken. To shed more light on the horrifying last moments of Christine's life, "a piece of cloth was tied around the girl's neck and secured with…a slip knot." The cloth was a strip torn from her own coat. Christine was a native of Chicago and had only recently enrolled at the University of Wisconsin–Madison with hopes of becoming a journalist. During her time in Chicago, she had modeled for department store catalogues. There was evidence left at the scene of the crime that gave hope to finding the murderer.

Some bloody clothing—including a man's handkerchief that was found under Christine's head and a broken umbrella that was stabbed into the ground next to her body—was sent to the FBI for further testing. The FBI testing didn't help discover the killer's identity at the time, and when the items were sent back to the sheriff's office, they were lost. With today's advances in technology and scientific understanding, it is unfortunate that we do not have some of these items. They certainly could have illuminated new suspects or convicted old ones. Police at the time thought her death could be connected to similar killings in the Milwaukee area. No conclusive connection could ever be made. The reason for her death and her murderer's identity remain mysteries to this day.

In November 1972, newspaper deliveryman Arthur Foeste was making his rounds just before six o'clock in the morning a few days before Thanksgiving. While making his delivery to the Joyce Funeral Home at 540 West Washington Avenue, he discovered a body slumped on the floor in a front hall. The body was that of Mark Justl, age twenty-eight, who had been strangled to death. Marv Balousek, author of *101 Wisconsin Unsolved Mysteries*, wrote that Mr. Justl had "a black eye, a bruised mouth and a bleeding wound on the head from a fist or an unknown object." He also had fingernail scratches on his face and neck.

According to the *Wisconsin State Journal* in an article from December 8, "Detectives said the ransacked offices indicated either that Justl surprised one

Just beyond this very entry on 540 West Washington Avenue is where Mr. Justl's body was found. *Photograph by Noah Voss.*

or more burglars on his arrival home, or that he had been killed for another reason and the premises ransacked to make it appear a burglary attempt." Justl was seen at several businesses in the neighborhood on the night of the murder and returned home about 3:00 a.m. by himself. If it was burglary turned murder, the unidentified assailant only made off with "$10 petty cash from an upstairs desk, seven bottles of liquor from a basement storage locker belonging to a second-floor resident, and Justl's large black shiny wallet."

Though she never looked into it further, one neighbor reported to police that she heard a scuffle in the hall followed by a car leaving the premises at about three o'clock in the morning that same night. The mysterious murder remains such to this day. However, there was a confusing development in the case only five months later. Justl's roommate was found in the woods of Picnic Point on the shore of Lake Mendota. Linford Smith was dead from an apparently self-inflicted gunshot to the head. A .38-caliber pistol was found near the body. Police had originally "quizzed" the roommate on three separate occasions, including using a polygraph test, which he passed. Again, the state's crime agency lost or destroyed key evidence that today could have been tested for additional leads in the case. This was not the first time someone had taken his own life on Picnic Point.

It is believed that August Kutzbock walked off Picnic Point into the freezing November waters of Lake Mendota. He had been recently removed from the 1868 construction project on the capitol and replaced by Stephen Vaughan Shipman—a demotion that Mr. Kutzbock was said to have taken very hard. He had already invested much of his time in the project and was nearing his own final view for the dome portion of the capitol.

A short mystery from 1976 led police down a path of few clues. It was July 21 when the "charred and decomposed remains" of Debra Bennett were found. A land assessor happened upon the body in a gully just west of Madison. The cause of death was undetermined by autopsy, though it was estimated that she had been dead for approximately ten days or longer. Debra had been evicted from her Madison apartment recently and was staying at the Cardinal Hotel in downtown Madison. The next lead was to go nowhere, but it did spark speculation among investigators and fear among hotel employees.

The Cardinal Hotel received Debra's room key in the mail. The police followed up, but no new clues were found. Was the key simply found by a Good Samaritan and returned? Perhaps the murderer was toying with police? Three weeks had passed since her body had been found when the key turned up. It was the last clue to be discovered.

To meet our next mystery, we must rise to the occasion. To be specific, rise eighteen thousand feet on June 24, 1978, when we join some confused pilots. Thanks to Allan Hendry of the Center for Unidentified Flying Objects (CUFOS) and its publication, *International UFO Reporter* (*IUR*), this case was thoroughly researched and investigated at the time. CUFOS was founded by Dr. J. Allen Hynek, an internationally renowned UFOlogist with more than forty years of experience.

The top of the capitol, shown today, remained unfinished when Mr. Kutzbock was removed from the project. *Photograph by Noah Voss.*

The Madison Airport Tower received a call from the Madison Fire Department about some lights doing circles in the clouds. A Madison resident had called the fire department. Unable to identify the lights, the fire department in turn called the airport. The Madison Fire Department was recorded as saying, "It looked like a spotlight searching the sky, only weaker, and located just in the cloud layer." Controller Joan M. was working the tower that night and began looking into the report. After all, it was her job to bring the airplanes safely through the air space around Madison. The time was now 10:45 p.m. If there was something in the clouds, she needed to know about it. Joan's investigation prompted her to call another airport:

MAD: You don't have anything over Madison anywhere, do you, doing circles?
AUR: No, we don't have anything over Madison, doing circles.
MAD: Well, I tell you—
AUR: We've got some weather out there that's doing circles.
MAD: Oh. Would you believe I've got a UFO?
AUR: Well…
MAD: —that I can see?
AUR: Let's take a look at him. Where's he at?
MAD: He's just south of the field and he is—uh—he's doing circles very fast in a small…looking out one window. I can't see "him," I see this light.
AUR: OK, just a second, let us flatten out the other radar a second. You say he's how far south of the field?
MAD: Well, he looks like he's over the marker, but…you know, it's just a light doing a circle.
AUR: Probably just a bunch of little greenies out there, eh?

The controllers at AUR wanted to find other witnesses and hopefully gain some more data on what might be going on. There was a multi-engine aircraft located just south of Madison on a northwest heading:

AUR: Have you got your landing lights on?
PIL (PILOT): Negative.
AUR: Do you see any kind of unusual lights ahead of you?
PIL: Yes, sir, I've got a bright light right at my 10:30, 11 o'clock position that just seems to be hovering out there.
AUR: Any idea of the altitude?
PIL: Yes, sir, the same altitude I am.
AUR: OK, I've got a VFR [Visual Flight Rules] target at 2 o'clock at about 6 miles westbound squawking 1200 which would indicate a lower altitude.
PIL: Uh, this isn't at 2 o'clock; this is between 10:30 and 11:00.
AUR: OK, we just had a call from Madison tower; they're a little concerned about lights out there. They're obviously seeing what you are. Any idea what it is?
PIL: No, but you're starting to worry me. I hope this isn't one of those—uh—UFOs.

More data was coming forth. There was now another witness—a pilot mid-flight. On radar, a "possible stationary target was found at the plane's 10:30 position three miles distant." The pilot visually plotted the location of what he was seeing with where the radar return was located. The controllers were not yet willing to accept the radar return. They were "uncertain," as some natural conditions such as thermal inversions can create a radar return even when there is no object. These thermal inversions, however, typically have a very distinctive return and are not easily mistaken for an aircraft. The pilot was recorded as having eighty-five hundred flight hours and a first-class medical certificate with no waivers and was thirty-two years old at the time of the sighting. The time was now 10:49 p.m. as the observations continued:

> PIL: *I have some lights racing around on top of the clouds down here.* [There were no clouds blocking his view of the other light.] *I saw them below me and I have a light that is making a circle…It's doing a 360° circle about once every 5 or 6 seconds.*
> AUR: *Could that possibly be a searchlight on the ground showing up through the clouds?*
> PIL: *That is a distinct possibility, yes, sir. The stationary target is now moving closer to me.*

So there were two lights, one most likely becoming an IFO, or Identified Flying Object—simply a searchlight. The other light remained a UFO to a pilot who was documented by investigators of the time as "good-natured, [with an] earthly self-presentation and professed no previous interest in UFOs."

The time was 10:53 p.m. as their attention was drawn to the west-northwestern light:

> PIL: *You mean to tell me that you got nothing on radar down there at all?*
> AUR: *We're getting a lot of temperature inversion in that area. We are painting no targets whatsoever. There are no airplanes in that area.*
> PIL: *Tell you what, this ain't no-o-o weather inversion.*
> AUR: *OK, could it possibly be a weather balloon?*
> PIL: *Not unless a weather balloon lights up like a 10,000-candle light.*
> AUR: *OK, you're sure it is an object and not a light reflecting off a cloud or anything.*
> PIL: *Affirmative.*

AUR: Have you tried moving your position in the cockpit to see if that changes the position of the target? Perhaps you're getting a reflection of some type in the cockpit.
PIL: Sir, I'll try it. [Later] I just woke my passenger up and he sees the object, too, and it is not a reflection.

Thanks again to the UFOlogists of the time, we have much more specific data about the people involved. For example, when the passenger was awakened by the pilot, he reported seeing the "light out of a rear window… behind the pilot's seat." We also learn that the passenger was a customer of the pilot's charter flight business; he was thirty-six years old and an "extremely wealthy business man from Phoenix." When the pilot was asked how the businessman responded, he indicated that the passenger was "upset by the experience."

I wrote the following in my book *UFO Wisconsin: A Progress Report* about the unusual movement and positioning of the light in this exact case:

The object moved about the plane as they continued their steady course and to follow in their terminology it helps to visualize an analog clock in your mind, one with only the hour hand. Moving from the pilots "ten-thirty position at an estimated 15 miles" away to as close as two miles from the plane. Now considerably closer to the plane it then "dropped back to the 9 o'clock position" and again moved out to a 15 mile distance. When the pilot estimated the distance of the light to be "15 miles" there was still no radar confirmation made. This may have been due to the "large area of temperature returns" in the immediate vicinity. It was recorded the plane in question here can only "be seen on radar…because he is equipped with a transponder." What's more peculiar, is this all happened within approximately just one minute. Then the object lost an estimated 500 feet of altitude and moved up to their "11 o'clock position."

The time was now 10:56 p.m.:

AUR: Any chance that it's an aircraft with lights?
PIL: Negative, sir, negative—uh…uh—it's a white light and it's changing to—it, it's a weird color. It's alternating colors so I would have to say it's not an aircraft, negative.
AUR: I take you don't want to make any guesses as to what it is.
PIL: I may be dumb but I'm not stupid.

AUR: [Laughter in background] *Uh, roger. Does it pose any possible threat to you?*
PIL: I would say—uh—no, sir. I'm getting some turbulence right now. The object has faded now down into five distinct lights...uh, it's a white light with five red ones around it now.

The plane's location was now "fifteen miles northwest of Wisconsin Dells" and fully clear of the temperature inversions that were confusing earlier radar use. The tower confirmed "some type of non-transponding target." The pilot reported that the object was still following them in the ten thirty position, and the weather was now "quite clear: every star was seen in the sky."

AUR: Do you still have the target?
PIL: It went—uh—from my 10 o'clock over to my 2 o'clock and it's now hovering over there...when that baby took off, it took off.

A moment later, the pilot relayed that the UFO had jumped back to the original side of the plane. Of course, the plane had been "holding straight northwesterly course on autopilot," so the pilot and passenger were able to have a stable view. What's more interesting is that UFOlogists were able to ascertain from their investigation that the target "jumped" from "the left side of the pilot's position to his right and back again." Investigators documented that the controller noted this happening as the radar screen refreshed one full cycle—a "6-second sweep." Even more unusual was the fact that the UFO appeared on radar in five consecutive sweeps of the radar, except for the second. The controller had "never seen it appear and disappear so fast before."

The tower and pilot continue to work on the problem:

PIL: You know, if that is an illusion, I can see how somebody could be easily fooled by it.
AUR: Could you possibly turn off all your dash lights and external lights for a few moments to see if that does anything?
PIL: Sir, we already did that.
AUR: OK, so it's definitely not a reflection of any type off you—uh—off your aircraft.
PIL: Definitely not, sir.
AUR: Do you have the moon in sight?
PIL: Stand by. No, sir, no moon in sight.

AUR: Roger. Madison tower said that she could see you visually but—uh—she could still see you on radar, but she also picked up no targets on radar around you!
PIL: [Sarcastically] *How thrilling!*

At 11:05 p.m., the UFO "shot up in altitude to approximately 45 degrees above" the pilot. He went on to estimate that the UFO was now "six or seven thousand feet higher than him."

The time was now 11:09 p.m.:

AUR: OK, I've got a very possible target right over the Volk Airport.
PIL: Is that cotton-picker keeping pace with me at the same speed?
AUR: No sir, it appears to be stationary over Volk Field right at this time. I'll put him at 12 o'clock at seven miles.
PIL: Target's moving closer.
AUR: Roger, the target I have is stationary, you're heading right for it… possibly, maybe, 10 degrees off to the right of you—dead on course.
PIL: Target's coming in closer.
AUR: That target is definitely growing [on radar]—*uh—I don't know exactly what would cause that unless it was a change in relative position. It's almost the same size as your aircraft. It would now be about one o'clock at three miles.*
PIL: Yes, sir, it's getting very bright and turbulence here. [The pilot would later tell IUR that he was getting "white caps on his coffee."]
AUR: Would you like to change course?
PIL: Uhhhh…I think it's just the weather. Let's go and find this thing out.
AUR: OK, down to about one-thirty and two miles.
PIL: Yes, sir. Still got it at my 12 o'clock position at about that. I'm not painting any weather in this area, and I'm in clear air, but I'm getting moderate to—uh, um—lightly—um—you know, about moderate turbulence.
AUR: Roger, we—we've—uh—been having—uh—turbulence reports from that area all day long from North Central jets at 20 to 24,000.
PIL: [Sarcastically] *Good.*
AUR: OK, you should be at about 2 o'clock at two miles.
PIL: Whatever it is, it's lit up like a Christmas tree.
AUR: I now show you having passed the target I was painting.

The pilot had taken his plane directly underneath the UFO. His up-close view of the object allowed for additional descriptions, "small red lights held their positions on the surface" of the "oval-shaped form." As he neared the UFO, he thought the size was "half the full moon's diameter," whereas when he was farther away earlier in the night, he estimated the relative size to that of a "large star."

AUR: Where is the target now, sir?

As the pilot made it completely under the UFO, he was able to take his focus off the situation and contact tower control:

PIL: Well, right now, I'm in extremely smooth air and—nothing. Nowhere.
AUR: OK, you've lost the target now?
PIL: Completely.
PIL: I'm glad you finally got something on radar, I thought I was losing my mind.
AUR: Well, sir, in this area, I picked it up…I'm now also picking some other things that could be temperature inversion; however, that one was pretty steady and it did certainly correspond to your position.
PIL: Where's the Air Force when you need 'em?
AUR: That was right over their base.
PIL: Ah, ha! The "secret weapon!"
AUR: Yep, may be. The only problem being, if that was—uh—possibly a military-type aircraft that was out flitting around and—uh—was messing around in VFR conditions, I would have been picking up reflected radar signals from it, and it would have been moving along with you; however, when I was calling the target out to you, it appeared to be stationary.
PIL: That's the way it appeared to me, too, and I kept moving in close on it and I would get up there and the lights would become very distinctive and it would start to depict this shape and it was a coincidence, I'm sure, and my imagination, but every time we got close to it, we picked up turbulence.
AUR: Roger.
PIL: Believe me, I'm going to talk myself out of this yet!
AUR: No need to do that, you saw what you saw, that's all there is.

For space's sake, we'll jump ahead in the transcript of their conversation:

AUR: Do you plan on making a report of this to any type of agency?
PIL: [Hesitantly] Well! I don't know about that…do you?

AUR: Well, I reported it to my supervisor and—uh—that's all I'm required to do. I didn't see it so I wouldn't be of much value to anybody who would care to investigate a situation like this. However, if you'd like corroboration as far as radar reports and stuff—uh—that could probably be arranged.
PIL: Well, I'll think about it.

UFOlogists investigating this case documented that controllers Glen W. and Wayne N. were both witnesses to the night's events. Glen was thirty-two years old and had eight years' experience on the job. Both controllers reported their unique night to their supervisor, who took no further known action.

AUR: If you do make a report to anybody, and they want to know what was seen on radar, they just have to make an inquiry to the Chicago Air Traffic Center and mention the time and date and they'll be able to find out what patrol I was working.
PIL: OK, just give them time of day and I don't have to give them your name?
AUR: [Chuckling] *Oh, they'll find that out easy enough.* [Says flight number], *now direct all-clear on course. Contact Minneapolis Center on 125.3—good night, and have a good trip.*
PIL: 125.3, good night now.

This mysterious UFO event doesn't quite end there. The controllers at Aurora were contacted by North Central passenger flight 577. During that conversation, the controllers asked if the North Central pilots had ever experienced anything like what they were just listening to unfold:

PIL: Uh, could be, years and years ago, that I had this happen. Are we going to be flying in that area where we saw this? We'll be apparently northeast of it, is that right?
AUR: Yeah, you'll be northeast of it. The last place that we saw it was right over Volk Airport.

Interestingly, the controllers had radar confirmation again on the UFO. They recorded that it was remaining motionless at the time. I absolutely love that the controllers offered flight 577 a course correction with itinerary that would take them to the UFO:

PIL: We—uh—we don't want to take any chances like that, but—uh—maybe we can pick it up. Sometimes we can pick up other aircraft on our 50-mile scope so we'll see if we can pick it up on our scope, too.

AUR: Roger, the area that I had the target in I'm getting temperature inversion off the southeast of it; however, the target that I called out for him that corresponded to the position is still within a mile of the same relative spot right over Volk Airport.

PIL: Very interesting.

The time was now 11:31 p.m., and flight 577 was only 27.5 miles out from the UFO on radar:

PIL: I'm almost sure I can see a light over there.

Investigators documented flight 577 pilot's description of the faint light as "changing different colors."

At 11:50 p.m., the object reportedly "faded" away, and no other sightings were documented.

Investigators from CUFOS recorded that the McCoy Army Air Force Base and the Army National Guard training site were "contacted to see if any of their operators could have accounted for the sighting." There were no explanations forthcoming. The only way CUFOS was able to investigate and document this UFO experience was because controllers Glen and Wayne called them directly to file a report. If they hadn't, this would have likely been a family story told only in confidence.

Back when Saturday newspapers in Madison sold for thirty cents, the headlines once again ran red. It was 1982, and another murder mystery was unfolding. The most recent victim was twenty-three-year-old UW-Madison college student Donna A. Mraz. Donna was on her way home from "the BitterSweet Restaurant, 117 State St., between 11 and 11:30" in the evening.

According to the *Wisconsin State Journal*, Donna lived on Van Hise Avenue but never arrived home. The only witness to her final steps was a student watching out the window of his Breese Terrace apartment. Donna was walking just north of Camp Randall Stadium when she was attacked. The witness was alerted by Donna's single scream. The police reporter, Marvin Balousek, wrote in a newspaper article that "according to his roommates, the UW student walked to his apartment window and saw Ms. Mraz fall." He ran outside and saw that she had been stabbed. Donna was able to stumble some thirty feet from where the police determined she was attacked before

State Street, facing toward the capitol, would have appeared the same when Donna Mraz was walking home in 1982. *Photograph by Noah Voss.*

she fell to the ground. When the student got to her, he found "a deep wound on her left arm stretched from shoulder to elbow and penetrated nearly to the bone and the student also saw dampness caused by blood on her chest." The student unfortunately didn't see anyone else when he initially looked out his apartment window: "She was running and she just hit the ground, bleeding everywhere, from the chest and her arms. I didn't see anyone; she didn't say anything." The student ran back inside, where he called the police and returned to Donna with another man. She lay bleeding to death on the cold cement. After placing a blanket around her, the student reported that "he heard her gagging and tried to resuscitate her." The Madison Fire Department paramedics were on the scene within three minutes and "spent 20 minutes at the scene, trying to stabilize the woman's condition, before taking her to the University Hospital," where she later was pronounced dead. The police had very few leads.

There had been several sexual assaults in the university campus area, some that included a knife-wielding, unidentified assailant. There was also the unsolved murder of Christine Rothschild, who was stabbed fourteen times in the downtown area in 1968. Police even went so far as to use controversial hypnotic regression, hoping that some witness might have seen more than he or she could consciously remember. Despite compiling a rough police sketch of a bearded man seen near the stadium that night and offering a $10,000 reward, the police were running out of avenues to pursue. A new lead was to come in November of the same year.

Donna Mraz's body was exhumed for "tests related to the investigation," according to university police officials. Detectives wanted to compare dental casts of Donna to "bite marks on a possible suspect." The suspect was already serving a sentence in prison, but no definitive conclusion could be made with the evidence. The man later died in prison, and no other suspects were found.

Our next mystery comes from 1988, when again a UFO was sighted above the "Mad City." I personally spoke with the witness, who shared that he was hanging out in his room in a downtown apartment. It was a nice day, and the window was open, and that's where John sat watching the day go by. Something in the sky caught his attention. It was a bluish gray object that was "nearly invisible to my naked eye," he shared. John estimated the size as "not quite…the size of a dime on its side at arm's length." For all you aspiring UFO witnesses, that is a great way to give scale to something you are viewing in the sky. It may initially sound overly complicated; however, all things being relative, this method helps give scope to a situation difficult for investigators to, well, accurately investigate after it is over.

Let's run through a quick mental exercise. If a 747 jet airliner is sitting on the runway, you might easily be able to identify points that anyone can later compare for size, such as the end of the runway to the ninth light. Using that information in relation to where the witness was can divulge some helpful data to the intrepid investigator. When in the wide-open sky, the 747 has nothing else an observer can compare it to. This is called losing perspective. A way to gain some perspective is to imagine that you are holding something in your hand at arm's length. This is not a precise science, mind you, just something that investigators can later use as a single data point among many to estimate the size and potential location of an object. For example, a 747 jet airliner may be obscured by one basketball held at arm's length if you view it flying one thousand feet overhead. That same 747 may only be covered by a single pea held at arm's length if viewed from two miles. Take that same jet and place it forty thousand feet up (over six miles), and from the ground it quickly begins to look like a star in the night sky, or perhaps the size of a grain of rice held at arm's length.

Back to John in 1988. The object he was trying to identify, running through all the usual aerial objects, was turning up nothing. He told me that at first he "thought it was one of the small scratch marks in [his glasses] lenses…but after a couple of movements" of the glasses and his head, the UFO was still there. John was able to view the UFO for only about fifteen seconds as it made unusual "zigzagging" movements, until it darted across the sky and out of sight. He again shared a great piece of eyewitness data, saying that there was a vapor trail behind the UFO "about a yard long at arm's length." John didn't brush this off lightly, as he had the classic response of all the hairs on his body standing on end.

Taken by itself, this UFO report is certainly not the most sensational. If we begin to look at a wider set of data points, even if we only look statewide right here in Wisconsin, things get a bit more intriguing. In August 1985, a UFO with a searchlight was spotted one night by over two dozen witnesses from cities in six states, including Western Madison. Again, several of those sightings detailed zigzagging movements. On June 14, 1997, a couple enjoying an afternoon by Lake Michigan spotted something doing "crazy spirals" until it "dropped out of the sky." In June 1998, an Elmwood, Wisconsin family stopped their car to watch "four red balls of light…zigzag around" a "bright white ball of light" for about five minutes. On April 7, 2001, over Milwaukee, witnesses initially thought they were watching a meteorite burn into the atmosphere until the object "moved in a zig-zag like fashion across the sky directly overhead to the western horizon and then disappeared." Another UFO report from Milwaukee occurred in March of the same year, when an anonymous witness watched a "can-shaped object…glowing" as it "moved really fast going left to right about 3 feet at a time." On February 12, 2002, some friends were shooting baskets in their backyard at about 8:00 a.m., when they noticed a UFO making "a series of darts across the sky" for several minutes, until it "darted off east." On January 11, 2004, Trisha N. was letting her dogs out for the evening when she reported several objects that she thought were airplanes, until they stopped midflight and "did a zig-zag shape flying up towards space." On November 13, 2004, Diana watched a UFO performing "acrobatics around the sky…at unlikely speeds"; it would stop and hover at times. On July 5, 2005, guests at the Pfister Hotel in Milwaukee watched as an object "swooped in one direction, then slowly lost velocity until it came to a halt, then swooped in the opposite direction."

Author John Peyton Cooke wrote *Torsos*, a dramatic true-life crime novel based in part on the following mystery from Madison. He would have been made aware of it from his time working in Madison typing police reports.

Our mystery begins as the owner of Good N' Loud Music was doing some renovation repairs in the basement. After removing some exhaust ductwork, he moved his light up the chimney, revealing, to his horror, human remains. Thanks to Marv Balousek of *101 Wisconsin Unsolved Mysteries*, we know that the owner notified the police. Dane County coroner Ray Wosepka investigated the remains for the police. Ray told the *Wisconsin State Journal*, "We will be using the crime lab, anthropologist, and everybody else we can think of to give us some help." The remains were greatly decomposed, and any initial information was only gathered from the clothes. The remains were in a "sleeveless paisley dress with matching belt, button-down oxford shirt, White Stag brand shaggy-pile sweater, socks, and low heeled pointed shoes." Though no identification was found, an extra pair of socks was carried and no underwear worn. Detectives went to work identifying the remains.

Then, the forensic tests turned up the next mystery: "she" was a "he"! Though the remains wore women's clothing, the tests concluded that they belonged to a tall, slender man. Detectives searched through missing persons files and worked every theory. There were several, including that the man may have been trying to burglarize the business by gaining access through the chimney. This was later ruled out due to the clearly unacceptable size of the access point. Even more diabolical was the theory that perhaps the man in women's clothing had picked up a man, who, finding the truth of his date's orientation, lashed out, disposing of the body in the chimney. More innocent theories included Madison's less-than-innocent nearby annual Halloween celebrations. Perhaps the man was a partygoer for the fall festivities, dressed in female costume. Despite years of effort, no additional leads were to be had.

The case garnered national television attention, and the Smithsonian Institute even completed a facial reconstruction of the remains. Nothing more of this mystery is known to this day.

WESTERN MADISON

Forest Hill Cemetery on Madison's West Side has a long and varied history. Forest Hill was established in 1858, only two years after Madison officially transitioned from a village into a city. The cemetery held 148 acres of rolling, sparsely wooded, tombstone-topped trimmed grass. Countless local celebrities can be found here, resting alongside several nationally famous folks, Civil War soldiers and bodies originally laid to rest in completely different cemeteries. Though the Forest Hill Cemetery staff was not able to verify this, it is rumored that the oldest marked tombstone has a birth year of 1764. If true, Lydia Colburn passed away in March 1852, after eighty-eight years of life. Lydia would have left behind a population of 1,525 living Madisonians and joined an unknown populace of ancients buried through the region. One can find clues to these ancient people who called this land home long before 1852, if one knows where to look.

Earthen and effigy mounds are some of the physically largest clues left behind from a nation of people about whom not everything is known. Effigy mounds are earthen structures mounded up above the height of the surrounding land and then into the shape of an animal or mythical creature. These mounds are not found anywhere else in the world in the same concentrations and numbers as in Wisconsin. The people who are believed to have created them are estimated to have lived here between 800 BC and AD 1200, according to Robert A. Birmingham and Leslie E. Eisenberg in their book *Indian Mounds of Wisconsin*. About twelve to ten thousand years ago, Paleo-Indians are thought by most to have entered the Wisconsin area.

A map from 1911 showing West Madison. The capitol is on the right, a large square with a dark *X. WHS-41578.*

They are believed to have subsisted on the increasing vegetation as the once glacier-covered land became green again. If they were lucky enough to have a successful hunt, they would have feasted on the larger ice age animals such as mastodon, woolly mammoth and, of course, bison. Over the course of the proceeding few thousand years, the ice retreated farther north, allowing the climate to become warmer and the environment drier. This time is referred to as the Archaic Period.

The people of this period would have been able to consume a wider variety of vegetation than their ancestors. The people of the Archaic Period would have also begun to find the more familiar deer and bear in the region. Jumping further down the Madison area timeline brings us to about three thousand years ago.

The forests had generations of glacier-free life. This allowed the forests to become large, lush creatures unto themselves, hence the name for this time: the Woodland Period. Vegetation and wildlife were always plentiful. This allowed the people to peacefully gather more than ever before. The surplus of food allowed the people to avoid confrontations often generated by lack of food. It is speculated that before this time in history, food and needed resources were scarcer. Building on that logic, the people of those earlier times were perhaps more inclined to protect valuable hunting and foraging grounds at all costs. During the Woodland Period, it's believed that they began to live in large groups or tribes. Hunting with advanced weapons such as the bow and arrow became the norm. We know the people who lived during this time as the Mound Builders. They built many mounds on the very same ground that much of Madison now covers. Between then and the Mississippian Period that began about two thousand years later (or one thousand years ago), we start to see larger-scale cultivation and a complex network of trade that is thought to have reached to at least the Atlantic Ocean and the Gulf of Mexico.

The Mound Builders are thought to be the ancestors of at least some of the more modern Native Americans. Some of the elders of the Ho-Chunk Nation speak of the Mound Builders as their own ancestors. Before European explorers traveled through the area, the Fox and Sauk tribes were also inhabiting areas of what would become Wisconsin. It is likely that these people would have passed through the Madison area, too.

With Madison's population today at 233,209, there's not much room left for mounds. At the peak, perhaps fifteen or twenty thousand mounds dotted the countryside. It is estimated that today four thousand remain. Many of these large structures that consisted of shaped and formed piles of dirt and other natural materials were most likely used for ceremonial purposes, including burials. The area now enclosed by Forest Hill Cemetery holds several well-preserved effigy mounds.

Panther Effigy Mound in Forest Hill Cemetery. (Foreground: head, bottom left; chest, bottom center; front leg, lower right, with body moving from bottom center to the center middle; second leg, off to the center right; and tail, center center.) *Photograph by Noah Voss.*

The boulder holding the mound's maker plaque in the foreground, with the mound in background. *Photograph by Noah Voss.*

One mound is in the shape of a goose that sadly lost its head during construction of the Illinois Central Railroad in the 1880s. Even with the damage, the goose figure remains a rare form of effigy mound. There are two other effigy mounds in the shape of panthers in the cemetery. Both creatures are believed to have been held in high regard by the Mound Builders. Indeed, the more historians dig through oral traditions, the more it deepens the mystery. Though most agree that the first European explorer visited Wisconsin in 1634, we have some details from very early in the 1800s. Army engineer and hardened adventurer Stephen H. Long is thought to have been one of the first explorers to document Wisconsin mounds. Though the mounds were thought by some natives of the area to have been territorial markers, most agree that the meaning was deeper. The panther mounds were also referred to as water spirits or lower world spirits. Perhaps this was the indigenous people of Madison's way of identifying some mysterious creature that was occasionally still sighted into the 1900s. If not, maybe it was nothing more than an older version of the more modern devil in their Earth Creator stories. The Mound Builders are thought to have formed the bird-shaped effigy mounds after their own upper world spirit. Frequently, this was called Dancing Man or Thunderbird, according what oral tradition remains. From what experts can tell of the Forest Hill area, there were once at least three more locations of linear mounds. The last time I visited these mounds, they were marked by a large boulder holding a small bronze plaque identifying them for visitors.

The indigenous people, who called Wisconsin home before it was named such, had their final resting places throughout the city of Madison. Even in more recent times, when the city outgrew the original village cemetery, the bodies were disinterred. In the process, many were moved to Forest Hill Cemetery. Those that could still be identified properly were placed near family members' plots when possible. There were, however, many remains from unmarked graves or from graves with markers that had only the simplest information, such as names or ages. These remains were moved to resting places with similarly obscure or simple markings. It is not uncommon for cemeteries to have numerous unmarked graves, especially those cemeteries that have been around long enough for time to have taken its toll. If you do visit, watch your step, as it is whispered that Forest Hill Cemetery contains unmarked graves. For those who are keeping a running tab and enjoy

The sign that greets visitors at the main entrance to the grounds. *Photograph by Noah Voss.*

Hollywood horror movies, there are a couple of things popularly believed to cause unhappiness in the afterlife, among them unmarked and unknown grave sites, disinterred remains and, of course, desecrated Native American holy ground. These are the things of which many movies have been made. I won't ruin the romantic mysticism associated with these beliefs with overhanded quantifiable data, so let's just leave it that the jury is still out on this theory.

Forest Hill Cemetery is also said by some to have a Lady in White. The Lady in White has become common enough to earn its own category among most ghost enthusiasts. Often found wandering through cemeteries or along lonely stretches of roadways, the Lady in White is reported to appear and disappear quite inexplicably. Some people have even allegedly gotten close enough to talk to this troubled spirit. Other reports from motorists speak of picking up a Lady in White in their car, only to have her disappear while driving down the road. The Lady in White spotted at Forest Hill Cemetery is seen in normal fashion to appear and disappear quite mysteriously. I am told that she wears a dated large hoop dress, and unfortunately I have yet to hear of any occurrences with more detail.

For those looking for a slightly more traditional tour, the Forest Hill Cemetery Committee of Historic Madison Incorporated has a "walking tour brochure" that can be found online or through contacting the committee directly. The Forest Hill Cemetery Office occasionally has a foldout walking brochure available during normal business hours that highlights some interesting history.

Beyond Forest Hill Cemetery, the earthen and effigy mounds once dotted most of the Madison area. Many sites were focused near the lakeshores. Many more spread far into the distant land, where suburbs eventually took over. Indeed, mounds may have been on the land where you're sitting right now! Much is left unknown and shrouded in mystery, including the exact location of all the mounds. Our next report is a great case in point of what can be, even when you don't think it possible.

A woman driving from the west side of Madison on Highway 12 saw something she never would have expected. Indeed, she only came forward to a trusted friend in the police department who kept her identity a secret. Why all the cloak and dagger? Perhaps you'd be hesitant to go public if you saw a lion strolling along a Wisconsin roadway. That is just what our next witness saw. She likely wanted to remain anonymous to save herself the ribbing that would undoubtedly follow coming forward with such a tale. Regardless, on July 29, 1998, the witness was driving down the highway when she saw

A female African lion prowls the grasslands. *Photograph courtesy of Schuyler Shepherd.*

something near the roadway ahead of her. What assuredly drew a second and third look of disbelief was clearly described as "a female African lion." In *Mysterious America*, author Loren Coleman documented that Sauk County sergeant Fred Coller knew the woman and said she was "very credible." She said it wasn't a puma or a cougar because it was more muscular and had a long tail with a puff on it. Now, on the surface, this may sound like an outlandish claim; however, this was not the first, nor last, odd creature sighting that the Madison area would have.

Earlier that same month, a woman with experience hunting big game out of state came face to face with what she described as a "female African lion." She had been investigating her property outside Lake Delton, Wisconsin, after a few of her calves had been mauled. She walked up to a ditch on her property, where she reported found the lion. The police apparently offered up other possibilities for what she saw. The witness retorted, "I know what I saw. I know it was a lion." Later in the month, and not far from Lake Delton, the Wisconsin Dells Ranger Station received several calls from people hearing lion roars. By August 3, another eyewitness report had been documented. Near the border of Sauk and Juneau Counties, a father and son watched in amazement as a "big cat" crossed their driveway. Before the lion scare was over, more than a dozen other sightings were made across the south central portion of the state, including the unusual mauling of several farmyard animals. While everything

The Old Sauk Road sign near where Thomas drove under the port-holed UFO. *Photograph by Dawson Black.*

from bigfoot to werewolves have been sighted countless times in and around the state of Wisconsin, kangaroo sightings have been the only ones so far to turn up a body of physical proof. Two kangaroo bodies were recovered after a rash of sightings swept through the state. Each time, there were more people preaching that it couldn't be what everyone was seeing than there were people actively investigating the sightings. I know because I was actively researching and investigating what the witnesses were reporting.

A similar scenario has more recently played out in Wisconsin with the sightings of cougars or cougar-like animals. Along with several paranormal investigators, I had been looking into the mysterious cases for years. During that time, the official stance of those in charge was that they were not cougars. Unfortunately for the witnesses, declaring this position was usually done down the nose and with a snicker. Then came the DNA proof that there was indeed a cougar in Wisconsin. Further tests of samples revealed that at least four cougars had been in Wisconsin. What's the point, right? Well, only that when presented with a mystery, it has been my experience that to discount any data, even testimony, without due diligence of research and investigation is to guarantee that you will miss out on something.

We turn from unexplained creature reports to mysteriously occupied UFOs. It is less often that a UFO sighting will include some being. That might be just what happened in 2003 on Madison's West side. Thomas E. was "driving west on Old Sauk Road."

A Madison population sign from early 2011 reading 208,054. A more recent census places current population around 233,209. *Photograph by Noah Voss.*

As many UFO reports go, Thomas noticed something in the February sky that drew his attention. What he initially thought "was a plane" he soon realized wasn't like anything he had seen before. As Thomas continued down the road, he drew closer to the object that now "appeared to be shaped roughly like a boat." Thomas crossed paths with the UFO, driving almost directly under it. With his closest view yet, he reported to my website, UFOwisconsin.com, that it seemed "stationary...30-40 feet in length, maybe 10-15 feet wide." The most startling observation was "lights or windows running along each of the sides...there appeared to be people in the windows." He was thorough enough to share that what gave him this impression was "at least black circles in the windows, which" Thomas "interpreted to be occupants." Thomas came off as an open-minded observer when he shared his experience to me through the website. He shared that maybe it "was a helicopter" but was confused to not see "any blinking lights and made no sound." With such a sight over such a populated area of Madison, surely there had to be other witnesses. The population in

2003 was about 208,054, which is a fair number of potential witnesses. A similar situation in which a large populace was actually looking up at the sky happened in Phoenix, Arizona. In 1997, a UFO passed over the city, and ten thousand people were estimated to have witnessed the unexplained object.

Jumping ahead to 2006, we find a middle-aged woman, a teacher who had "never seen a UFO before"; that is, before this night. On August 2, she noticed "three lights in a row: white, white, blue," and thought it was "an airplane, but the object circled in a way that an airplane cannot." She thought that it "moved more like a kite than a plane or helicopter"; however, she didn't think that was a likely explanation because "the lights were large enough that I doubt a kite could have held them at altitude." She went on to notice there was no sound, and "after about five minutes it disappeared behind the tree line." That was the last she saw of it.

Northern Madison

Disease. Healthy people becoming ill has been a mystery that remains today. Madison's north side has the Lake View Tuberculosis Sanatorium as a constant reminder of darker times. Tuberculosis, the white plague or consumption was known as such by those close to the suffering and dying. The disease earned its many names through its slow sickening symptoms, which included a chronic cough lasting weeks that would often contain bloody sputum, described in many documents to this day as "white, soft cheese-like," along with notable weight loss, night sweats, general fatigue and the risk that the infection could spread to nearly any part of the infected body. While tuberculosis is now less of a mystery, what the old, stately structure sitting atop a large grass-covered hill used to hold is mostly unknown to current city residents.

Sanatoriums were all too common from the late 1800s through 1943. In 1943, Albert Schatz's research led him to streptomycin, the first identified antibiotic that could be used to cure tuberculosis. Before this wonderful day of discovery, sanatoriums were the preferred method for coping with the disease. The sanatoriums were often built to catch the wind, offering cool, calming breezes of fresh air to their patients, along with plenty of sunshine. This meant that tops of hills were ideal locations when deserts were not available. The Lake View Tuberculosis Sanatorium was placed on one of Dane County's highest hills, with an elevation of 1,017 feet above sea level and about 150 feet above the immediate surrounding land.

The sign to the entrance of one Northern Madison community. *Photograph by Noah Voss.*

The first sanatorium was created in 1863 at Gorbersdorf in what is now Poland. It was thought that the fresh air of high altitude paired with good nutrition would help its patients increase their odds of beating the illness. The word "sanatorium" didn't come into use until 1904, when those experts in the field felt they needed a more accurate description. Working with the Latin *sanitas* for "health" and the Latin root *sano* for "heal" produced sanatorium. This is often mistakenly used interchangeably with sanitarium, which is typically a place that focuses on mental health.

The first sanatorium in North America was the Adirondack Cottage, finished in 1885. Built in Saranac Lake, New York, its function was a cross between sanatorium and sanitarium for some time.

The Lake View Tuberculosis Sanatorium on Madison's north side has been host to mysterious occurrences over the years. Its initial construction was finished in 1930, with a total capacity of 105 beds. Madison's population at the time was 57,899. The residents of Madison became a continuing and constant rotation of patients at the sanatorium. It housed many people with a wide variety of health issues until it closed its doors in 1966. Thanks to the National Register of Historic Places, the old sanatorium may be around for

Lake View Tuberculosis Sanatorium, April 2011. It now holds government offices. *Photograph by Noah Voss.*

many years to come. In 1993, the building was included on the registry. This listing will continue to attract attention to the forty-eight acres that helped many people over many years.

Reports of haunted hallways and ghost-riddled caves were murmured about by neighborhood schoolchildren. What were once witch-filled woods for one generation became Satanist sacrificing forests for another. I have personally spoken with people who heard odd noises when they were alone in parts of the building. They spoke of things moving on their own. These people had strong reservations about the place being normal but wouldn't go so far as to say that it was haunted. Most would say that others who worked there did believe there were ghosts on the premises. Other stories have come in from many corners, some sourced and some not: reports of deep voices in the nearby cemetery and woods; stories of psychics touring the grounds, picking up on all sorts of "negative" or "evil" energy or spirits. The most dramatic experiences I've heard about secondhand are people purporting to have had their hair pulled and faces slapped by disembodied hands.

One of several buildings that remain on the old Lake View Tuberculosis Sanatorium grounds. It is believed that this was used at one point as the nurses' dormitory, April 2011. *Photograph by Noah Voss.*

My own investigation of the grounds has turned up the sometimes-cited caves as being nothing more than what are more commonly referred to as pipe chases. Buildings of this era and design are often large campuses composed of several buildings on the grounds. Often connecting these different buildings are underground passageways that contain plumbing, electrical wiring, air-handling ductwork and heating and cooling systems alike. While certainly spooky, they are anything but unusual. I will confess that even though I may have spent much time here, perhaps in every room of several of the buildings, I have yet to experience anything that could not be explained.

During my lectures throughout the country, I often feel compelled to qualify such statements of "non-paranormal experience." For example, a family living in a home for ten years might have six odd experiences they cannot explain. The family members may attribute these unexplained experiences to a "ghost." To continue with this example, if I am able to investigate these reports for ten hours over the course of two nights, then that might be about average. Of course, this is not ideal, but for someone

The cemetery once on the Lake View Tuberculosis Sanatorium grounds, April 2011. It is now connected to a local church. *Photograph by Noah Voss.*

without a television show budget or a college grant, it's realistic. Just because I didn't experience anything unexplained in the ten hours I was present does not necessarily detract from the experiences of the people living in the home for the last ten years.

Back at the Lake View Sanatorium, the views can easily shift one's mind to the dark and stormy, obscuring all sorts of wrongdoings.

The sanatorium now houses less dramatic government offices. It is, however, still a massive structure sitting atop the highest hill in sight. It is flanked on one side with a small cemetery and, to the rear, Lakeview Woods. Lakeview Woods is part of the Dane County Park system and offers hiking trails open from 5:00 a.m. to 10:00 p.m.

I have been down these trails on several occasions, twice in a downpour. I have yet to come across any indications of ghosts, witches or Satanists. Though, as I said before, just because I have yet to come face to face with such things doesn't mean they don't exist. Another Wisconsin author, Michael Norman, mentioned something along the same lines to me once. His approach at the time was less about finding scientific answers or even

A Lakeview Woods hiking trail, part of the Dane County Park system, April 2011. *Photograph by Noah Voss.*

having a focus on paranormal theory. He seemed to appreciate the folklore aspect of saving a story from obscurity and for the ages.

Michael Norman and his co-author, Beth Scott, were pioneers in the paranormal field when they documented the rider of ghost hill in their book *Haunted Wisconsin*. The ghost story starts, as so many do, "at the stroke of midnight." Somewhere off an "old road" that ran from "Madison to Token Creek," it was said that a "lean figure clad in white" mysteriously appeared on the hillside. The figure rode atop a "pale horse," and it was reported that the dreadful duo could be "plainly" seen. The figure was trailed by "a white cape fluttering in the breeze." In 1936, a brave soul by the name of George Armbrecht was planning on spending the night on the hill with several friends. George, a Madison resident, survived the night but spoke of no unusual sightings. At least one old tale still gets spoken about; it claims the ghost rider was a murder victim. After having been robbed, the nameless man was said to have been killed. He was then cursed to wander the night, on the same ground he called his last, his horse rampaging ahead seeking the rider's revenge.

I have been watching for this cloaked creature on a white horse for over a decade now. I regularly pass through the area, sometimes at midnight. My research has thus far turned up several precise locations, depending on with whom you talk. It is somewhere on Madison's north side to be sure, but one sad report would have the hill a hill no more. It would seem that some believe the ghost hill died when the airport expanded, leveling much of the land that the mysterious midnight rider once called home. Our next mystery flew over the same hills that the midnight rider rode.

The *Wisconsin State Journal* and the *Capital Times* newspapers were both printing UFO reports of area residents. It was 1985, and a delta wing, or triangle-shaped, UFO was being witnessed by many. John was driving on Highway CV on Madison's north side when he saw "three white lights." He estimated that they were only thirty feet above a nearby farmhouse. As with so many UFO witnesses, we hear their normal train of logic: "At first I thought it was an airplane, then I thought it was a helicopter." For full disclosure, this area is in line with the end of the Madison Airport and does have much air traffic. The longer John watched, the more he had to admit that he "didn't know what it was." John was a brave witness, stopping his car and stepping out into the cool November air, affording him a clearer view of a "roughly triangular" shaped object. He noted that the "bottom sloped into contours," and there was no noise coming from the UFO. His experience was ended in the paper with him sharing, "I'm a little reticent to talk about it—I haven't even told my wife...It sounds so crazy." A very similar UFO was witnessed on the city's east side only days later the same month. That experience is included in the Eastern Madison chapter.

An artist's re-creation of a UFO. *Noah Voss.*

EASTERN MADISON

To reach our next mystery in Eastern Madison, we must start a few miles from the city and years before the mysterious events. It was January 21, 1968, when Shirley was driving toward Madison. She was heading home with a car full of young girls after a late dance recital nearby. Shirley and her friend in the passenger seat, Mrs. Knipfer, were interrupted by one of the girls in the backseat. She was watching a "large, round, dark-gray object" in the sky and wondered what it was. Shirley pulled the car to the side of the road so they could get a better look. As they did so, they became "very scared" at what they were witnessing. The emotions in the car escalated as the object "appeared to drop sparks and flaming debris" as it continued moving closer to the car. Between the confusion of what they were seeing in the sky and the screaming from the backseat, Shirley pulled the car back on the road and quickly headed toward home. The witnesses were able to give a great description, estimating the object to be the size of a "hot-air balloon" at a distance of "the top of a barn." They were nearing Mrs. Knipfer's home, and the UFO was still visible, seemingly following them. Shirley went on to share with investigators that she "could almost see the bottom of it," but the "sparks" emanating from it obscured a clear view. The UFO continued past as they pulled in the driveway of Mrs. Knipfer's place. The car full of frightened women watched the UFO disappear to the east. The sightings that evening weren't over.

Reports of the UFO came from the Berge Farm, as well. Sheriff's Deputy Robert Shaffer and three "neighboring youths" were all at the Berge Farm.

Additional rumors of something that may have crashed to the ground were spread about. Shirley told investigators that "someone went to the Berge Farm and did see something on the ground there." As of yet, my own investigations into these reports have not been illuminating. I am desperately interested in whether it was a small piece of the UFO that fell or perhaps even the wreckage of an entire UFO.

It has been speculated that this UFO sighting from 1968 and the subsequent debris may have found their way to Warren Smith. Mr. Smith was an investigative journalist from Iowa who had a passion for the unexplained. Sadly, Mr. Smith passed away in 2003, and though I have written of his efforts before, I was not able to have the honor of meeting him personally. Through my research for this book, I was able to speak directly with Brad Steiger. Mr. Steiger is an internationally recognized researcher in the paranormal field and author/co-author of over 170 titles. He also happened to be friends with Warren Smith and was working closely with him at the time of the following experience.

With the help of many writers before me, this is what I was able to piece together thus far. Mr. Smith's passion drove him to Madison in the 1970s. The story begins at a Holiday Inn on the east side of Madison. I can only imagine that it was a dark and stormy night.

Mr. Smith checked into a room and quickly left, following up on a lead. His sources said that there was a farmer southeast of Madison who had in his possession a piece of a UFO. Meeting up with the farmer, Mr. Smith was given the "piece of metal" to have it examined, temporarily of course. He didn't know just how temporary the ownership would be.

Mr. Smith returned to the hotel, where he received a phone call from the farmer, who mentioned that "a fertilizer salesman had been out" to his farm. He went on to say that the salesman was "asking a lot about the UFO and the metal but not working too hard to sell fertilizer."

Internal alarms must have been going off for Mr. Smith, who, in true cloak-and-dagger fashion, took apart his hotel room TV in order to conceal the metal piece inside. The investigative journalist then left to meet with the frazzled farmer. Hopefully, he would be able to gather more details of the oddly behaving fertilizer salesman. You see, for a paranormal investigator, especially a UFOlogist, the MIB (or "Men in Black") are as elusive as a full-body specter appearing on video. The MIB have been described as showing up to UFO witnesses, even at times immediately following the experience, when the witness may have only just contacted an area UFOlogist. The characteristics of MIB are almost as varied as the people who report them.

There are some common threads to the encounters, however, including overt or obscure intimidation of the witness and portraying themselves as from a wide range of government organizations or the exact opposite, such as house painters, door-to-door salesmen or fertilizer salesmen. Often times, the MIB experiencers report very unusual demeanor and appearances from one or both of the MIB, which has led some to speculate that they might not be entirely human. Others speculate further that this is all the work of "spooks," a typically derogatory term for black-ops CIA agents.

Even among mysteries, there are those that remain more fringe than others. The Men in Black enigma is one such mystery. Many theories abound about the MIB's motivations, including active dissemination of disinformation on actual alien technology or simply complex advanced terrestrial technology. Others go further in speculating that perhaps they are softening the general populace by disseminating accurate alien information, leading up to eventual first contact. Whatever the reality behind the mystery, I'll admit that being this close to a possible encounter with the MIB must have been exhilarating for Mr. Smith. His exhilaration was soon to change.

Thankfully, Mr. Smith asked the "maids and hotel maintenance man to watch" his room while he was out. From them, he later learned that no sooner had he departed than others arrived. Two men approached Mr. Smith's vacant room and used a key to let themselves inside. This must have confirmed to Mr. Smith that he had drawn the attention of the rumored MIB. Once inside, the two men went through his suitcase and every other place they could find. The maid had let herself into the room, acting none the wiser, simply going about her normal cleaning and stocking duties. Meanwhile, Mr. Smith was confronted with a farmer who was convinced that he needed to give the piece of metal to the government.

Most certainly frustrated, Mr. Smith returned to Madison in order to fetch the piece of metal for the farmer.

Entering his hotel room, Mr. Smith was greeted by two strange men already inside. The story goes that one was comfortably lying on the bed, and the other was sitting at the desk. I can only imagine what the initial small talk was, as documents don't report it, before one of them directed, "You have something we want. A farmer gave you a piece of metal the other day. Our job is to pick it up." Perhaps they simply started in with that concise comment. Clearly, they had the upper hand and maybe the resources of a large organization backing them up. Mr. Smith is remembered by Brad Steiger as a "tough little scrapper" and had grown accustomed to being "threatened, insulted, and roughed up." (He had previously been a strikebreaker.) He was not going to be outdone that easily and demanded some identification from the two trespassers. One quickly retorted, "Name the agency and we'll produce it." The other chimed in without missing a beat, "Would you like Air Force, FBI or maybe NORAD?"

In an unusual twist in an already unusual experience, they ended up in the hotel coffee shop. The short of it is that Mr. Smith, for whatever reason, was told that "UFOs involve more than you or any civilian can realize." They're the most important thing and perhaps the greatest hazard that mankind has ever faced." A comment like that begs countless follow-up questions in my mind—not that additionally pointed answers would necessarily be forthcoming, but I would like to think that Mr. Smith tried. After all, he was an investigative journalist and very likely had much experience in the complex act of interviewing. I confess that while not the exact same scenario, I have had my own unique conversations with strangers over the years while researching and investigating the paranormal.

Mr. Smith's story wraps up after coffee. He returned to his hotel room and retrieved the piece of metal from its television hiding place. He handed it over to the two unidentified men and watched as they got into their car and drove off—but not before taking down the Illinois license plate. Mr. Smith followed that lead to the owner, residing in Chicago, with "CIA links." Following his experience, Mr. Smith drove straight back to Iowa. Obviously, his MIB encounter made a marked impression. Mr. Steiger recounted to me that he was "working in my attic study in Decorah when I heard footsteps coming up the stairs." Home alone at the time, and not expecting any company, he started downstairs to investigate. Mr. Steiger "found Warren half-way up the three flights to my study." Mr. Smith was "trembling, shaking like someone who had undergone violent trauma." Mr. Steiger went on to say that "it took me quite some time to calm him enough to tell me what happened." It was as I documented in the previous experience. Mr. Steiger closed the interview with the words planted by the MIB upon their departure from Mr. Smith, "For your good…your family's good…your country's good…and the good of your world, watch your step."

When you find yourself in the situation Mr. Smith was in, you don't always react like you should—or at least how you hope you might.

I myself have made many public appearances throughout the year. I'm in front of countless people at book signings, lectures and conferences and during research for my next project and investigations into varying reports. Through these, I have been approached by thousands of people sharing their experiences and asking every question possible. A few specifically stand out and may relate to the story at hand. For a brief example, while working my table of wares at a conference in Wisconsin, I was approached by an unassuming gentleman.

I was the keynote presenter, along with Kevin Lee Nelson, and we had yet to go on stage. A man in perhaps his early fifties approached from the side and rear of the table. The table was nearly up against a wall. Of course, time has taken the precise words from my mind; however, the conversation started well within my personal space. That is to say, the man reached his hand out to get my attention. I turned to face him, and he sort of slurred in a raised tone, "Say, you're into all that UFO stuff, right?" I agreed with some long-winded and probably annoying answer of "I do research, investigate and write about unidentified flying objects, among other things, yes!" I've been told I speak with a leaning to E-prime and always aim to be semantically correct, so yes, that is how I actually talk. I didn't get to fully answer his question, however. He either ascertained that I was saying yes before I finished or already knew who I was and that, indeed, I was into all this "UFO stuff." He stepped further into my personal space and then some. I remember thinking things had just gone from eccentric, odd and harmless to aggressive in an instant. I recall that I could not only smell his breath but also feel the warm, moist air as it left his mouth. I noted that there was no scent of alcohol, as this wouldn't be the first time someone needed a drink to get through one of my presentations. He looked me in the eyes, and using proper grammar and full annunciation, strongly said, "You know people can just disappear when they go looking into the UFO phenomena" in a lowered voice. My internal thoughts were far from the words that came out: "Yeah, I suppose so." Turning to the side and stepping back, I tried to break the tension that I was feeling. I asked something like: "Have you ever seen a UFO?" The man replied with a no. Then I was pulled away by an attendee wanting an autograph (yeah, it happens). I remember turning to Kevin and telling him to "remember this." I wanted his opinion of the gentleman later but didn't want to advertise it to anyone else around. I turned to see where my MIB was and couldn't find him in the crowd. There were perhaps 250 attendees at that conference, and I didn't see him for the rest of the evening.

If I may be allowed to share this confession on top of my example, I've not shared this experience before with anyone but those closest to me in the paranormal field. There are many reasons I don't speak of this; foremost, I think it loses something in translation into words, whether written or spoken. Now, in my line of work, I experience people, places and mysteries that are odd. Most other people's odd is my norm. But this man's language, mood change and positioning in relation to my own person; the boldly appearing and disappearing; the personality change; the speech pattern change—the entire aura created an unusual experience that I don't lie awake thinking about but have yet to forget. I have always thought that those fully capable of taking a life aren't of the type to waste their time threatening one directly, at least not overtly or in an emotional outburst. Just letting someone else know that one has an entirely unique skill set to make a person "disappear" is almost a classy way to be threatened.

Now, this isn't the only time my life has been threatened, affording me the sometimes unique luxury of perspective. Those threats that are more emotional are therapeutic for the individual, and most psychologists would agree that they are rude but healthy. The threats I receive driven by ideology seem to be born out of my endeavoring for answers. My quest for knowledge in many dark corners somehow makes these individuals feel I should no longer be alive. This is sadly to be expected. I did feel the experience was perhaps similar enough to include for perspective on Mr. Smith's story. Whatever the intentions of my MIB, or the lack thereof, I hope they at least help show the scope of the reality in which a UFOlogist must maneuver. Our next mystery involves a young woman who assuredly had not lived long enough to make the enemies I seem to have made.

Julie Speerschneider was out at the 602 Club in Madison on the evening of March 27, 1979. She was said to have left the club on University Avenue, with intentions of walking to a friend's house. This was not the last time she was seen alive, but she was reported missing by friends and family shortly after. Those who knew Julie put up a $500 reward for information on her disappearance. A man whose name does not appear to be in public records came forward. He recognized Julie in the pictures released to the media. He told authorities that he had picked up Julie on Johnson Street as she hitchhiked. This was on the evening of March 27, the night she disappeared. The man with the car also reported that Julie was not alone but accompanied by an unidentified young man. He dropped the pair off at the intersection of Johnson and Brearly Streets. The next lead was not to come until April 1981, and it was a grim discovery.

The Yahara River connects several local lakes in Madison. In April 1981, sixteen-year-old Charles Byrd was in Madison hiking along the banks of the river. He happened upon something protruding from the ground. Upon further scrutiny, to his astonishment he discovered a human skeleton. Alerting authorities, the remains were later identified as belonging to Julie Speerschneider. Julie's friends and family finally had some level of closure

Sober' witness describes UFO

This UFO sighting is documented here in a re-creation from the *Capital Times* newspaper of November 1985. *Noah Voss.*

for their beloved, who would have been twenty-two years old. Unfortunately, the authorities were no closer to finding the mysterious murderer. Due to the decomposed state of the body, cause of death was never determined.

Three years later, in 1984, detectives followed up on another lead. A prisoner in Texas was busy confessing to many murders and may have been in the Madison area at the time of Julie's disappearance. Henry Lee Lucas and his accomplice, Ottis Tool, were interviewed. Henry Lee Lucas turned out to have been passing through Wisconsin in 1979 on his way to visit relatives in Minnesota. The lead dried up when Lucas, after confessing to hundreds of murders, recanted. No additional clues have been made public about the murder of Julie Speerschneider.

"We don't see many reports like this. But this woman sounded normal," police department spokesman Joe Durkin said. It was 1985, and Joe was speaking about a UFO report they had received that November. In fact, the UFO mystery had been playing itself out in all the local papers for the entire month, starting with sightings on Madison's north side. This most recent sighting was again documented in the papers. The *Capital Times* reported that the witness was driving down Milwaukee Street when she first noticed something in the sky.

Initially, the woman thought it might be a helicopter when it appeared as "three lights above a row of trees." At this point, it was just over the local Baptist church at about 11:00 p.m. Then the "craft" descended "towards a house on the north side of the street." She reported that it lowered to only "10 feet above the road." The witness pulled the car over and thought she was going to see it "crash into the house," never taking her eyes off the lights. Then the UFO made a "sharp and graceful 90-degree turn just short of the curb." Moving toward the woman in her parked car, she said it rose "slightly in the middle of the block. Ascending straight up, several feet in front" of her car, it just avoided hitting the power lines. As it moved through this last area, it was partially illuminated by the streetlight. The woman added more details: "The craft is triangular, about 12 feet in length and black. A light shines from the narrow nose." The witness went on to speculate for investigators that the shape was "too trim for a person to be comfortably seated" inside. Further details included a "wide silver streak" that "extends from the nose to the tail" but was missing wings, propellers or visible engines. To make the sighting more mysterious, she said, "The craft moves in complete silence." At this point in the sighting, the craft began to head north, hovering "12 to 15 feet above a house." With what would have been the rear of the craft now facing her, she estimated the size as "about half the width of the roof" nearby. With the new perspective, she was able to observe that "two white lights flank the rear and a small red light is near the light on the right."

Now, of course, it doesn't prove or disprove anything precisely if the lights on a reported UFO fit what the regulations require. It should also be stated that this UFO was not described as regulations dictate for anti-collision lights, though similarities could be made. The FAA (Federal Aviation Administration) regulates the anti-collision lighting system on aircraft. Typically, lights in aviation red on left/port (that is left of pilot, in the pilot seat) and green lights on right/starboard (right of pilot, in the pilot seat). This is done for the simple fact of navigational visual markers. Ideally, one can tell whether an air vessel is coming toward or moving away from him by simply observing the locations of the lights with respect to each other. This same approach is used on water vessels. Though it technically could be possible for an aircraft to simply turn off its anti-collision lights, it is against regulations. The FAA regulation 91.209(b) "requires that an aircraft's anti-collision lights be turned on once that aircraft's engine is started for the purpose of air navigation." Also, the anti-collision light regulations put forth by the FAA vary from year of manufacture and size of aircraft. Now, an avid believer in extraterrestrial sources would postulate that the craft could simply mimic our terrestrial regulations. I would put forth that the same technique could probably be used on our own government's advanced technology projects. Whatever you believe, I'll include for your own UFO-hunting adventures the current accepted configuration of a terrestrial aircraft lighting system.

The witness gathered much information before her sighting was over, detailing "rectangular white lights" that flashed and blinked in "rapid succession." The final observation she made was that the movement of the lights seemed to "give it a flying saucer appearance." By this time, the enormity of what she was experiencing began to sink in. Fear forced her back into her car and quickly down the road, leaving the mystery behind.

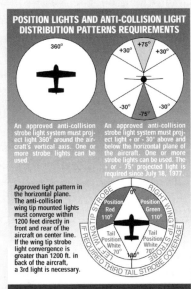

POSITION LIGHTS AND ANTI-COLLISION LIGHT DISTRIBUTION PATTERNS REQUIREMENTS

An approved anti-collision strobe light system must project light 360° around the aircraft's vertical axis. One or more strobe lights can be used.

An approved anti-collision strobe light system must project light + or - 30° above and below the horizontal plane of the aircraft. One or more strobe lights can be used. The + or - 75° projected light is required since July 18, 1977.

Approved light pattern in the horizontal plane. The anti-collision wing tip mounted lights must converge within 1200 feet directly in front and rear of the aircraft on center line. If the wing tip strobe light convergence is greater than 1200 ft. in back of the aircraft, a 3rd light is necessary.

ANTI-COLLISION and POSITION LIGHT REQUIREMENTS, LOCATIONS, & DISTRIBUTION PATTERNS

All aircraft must have an approved anti-collision light and position light system for nighttime operations. The position lights consist of an Aviation Red on the left side, an Aviation Green on the right and an Aviation White taillight (REF. FAR 23.1389).

The anti-collision lighting system is required under FAR PART 91.205(c). There are different requirements affecting different aircraft. These aircraft are categorized by the date of application for type certificate. Home built aircraft are determined by the date of issuance of the Experimental Operating Limitations. The different categories are as follows:

Aircraft for which type certificate was applied for after April 1, 1957 to August 10, 1971:
These anti-collision systems must produce a minimum of 100 effective candela in Aviation Red or White (REF. FAR 23.1397), 360° around the aircraft's vertical axis, 30° above and below the horizontal plane (REF. FAR 23.1401).

Aircraft for which type certificate was applied for after August 11, 1971 to July 18, 1977:
These anti-collision systems must produce a minimum of 400 effective candela in Aviation Red or White (REF. FAR 23.1397), 360° around the aircraft's vertical axis, 30° above and below the horizontal plane (REF. FAR 23.1401).

Aircraft for which type certificate was applied for after July 18, 1977:
These anti-collision systems must produce a minimum of 400 effective candela in Aviation Red or White (REF. FAR 23.1397), 360° around the aircraft's vertical axis, 75° above and below the horizontal plane (REF. FAR 23.1401).

Note: The position lights must be wired independently of anti-collision lights.

LOCATIONS ON THE AIRCRAFT FOR ANTI-COLLISION STROBE LIGHTS, TO COMPLY TO THE LIGHT PATTERN REQUIREMENTS

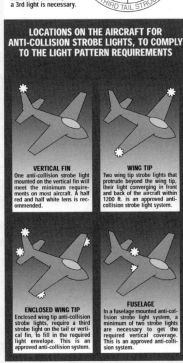

VERTICAL FIN
One anti-collision strobe light mounted on the vertical fin will meet the minimum requirements on most aircraft. A half red and half white lens is recommended.

WING TIP
Two wing tip strobe lights that protrude beyond the wing tip, their light converging in front and back of the aircraft within 1200 ft. is an approved anti-collision strobe light system.

ENCLOSED WING TIP
Enclosed wing tip anti-collision strobe lights, require a third strobe light on the tail or vertical fin, to fill in the required light envelope. This is an approved anti-collision system.

FUSELAGE
In a fuselage mounted anti-collision strobe light system, a minimum of two strobe lights are necessary to get the required vertical coverage. This is an approved anti-collision system.

INSTALLATION LOCATIONS

WING TIP:
The major difference in systems is the location of the strobe power supplies which can be mounted locally, one in each wing tip, or a single power supply can be mounted in the fuselage. Installation time can be greatly reduced if done in conjunction with an annual or one hundred-hour inspection. Properly installed power supplies and cabling are necessary for the safe operation of Whelen or any light systems.

FUSELAGE:
Fuselage mounted units can be either self-contained with the power supply and light head as one unit, or remote light heads run off a separate power supply. To meet the field of coverage, one must be on the top of the fuselage and one on the bottom.

VERTICAL FIN:
Finally, if applicable, a single anti-collision light can be mounted on the vertical stabilizer. It can be either a self-contained or remote light head depending on the aircraft.

Aircraft lighting outlined with visual shaded areas and attached descriptions. *Image courtesy of Whelen Engineering Co.*

The witness was so moved by her experience that she later phoned the police. Sergeant Ray Warner was quoted in the papers as calling himself a "born skeptic," though he had admitted to witnessing something in the sky he could not explain twelve years earlier. Of the witness, he shared, "She was real rational. She definitely saw something, I don't know what, but she saw something." The reporters from the *Wisconsin State Journal* investigated further: "Neither the tower at the Dane County Regional Airport nor an Air National Guard spokesman reported any unusual flying objects." Additional investigations revealed that Dane County Airport's radar was not actually in operation at the time of the sighting.

The next mystery begins on December 19, 1996, with a discovery in a lonely parking lot in southeastern Madison. Mark Meyer's 1978 Chevy Impala station wagon was found abandoned there. Mark, however, was nowhere to be found.

Mark had spoken with his daughter on the phone earlier in the month, on December 7. Things seemed fine—normal, in fact. She said they made plans for the upcoming holidays and that her dad was looking forward to a hunting trip he was soon to be taking. Mark had an apartment in Sun Prairie, just east of Madison. According to a neighbor just a few days after Mark spoke to his daughter on the phone, they walked in on "one or more burglars searching" through his place on Park Circle. Even odder is that another burglary was reported on December 10. Neither time were the burglars apprehended or identified, despite hundreds of interviews conducted by local law enforcement. The only thing authorities knew was that Mark was nowhere to be found.

Mark was a decorated Vietnam War veteran who, according to investigators, had been turning his life around from some hardships that included a drug possession charge two years earlier. The leads dried up, and Mark was still missing. Mark's remains an unexplained disappearance to this day. With a history of posttraumatic stress disorder and seizures, some speculated that if the worst happened, a body or note would have been found. Sun Prairie Police detective Bill Burton is quoted in Marv Balousek's book *101 Wisconsin Unsolved Mysteries* as saying, "This is the first one that I know of that someone has just disappeared like this. Normally they call eventually. Normally, there's some inkling they're somewhere. This guy, he just dropped off the face of the earth." Police eventually checked bodies that turned up as far away as Ohio in hopes that they could find some new lead to follow up on. No new leads have been forthcoming.

SOUTHERN MADISON

Though our next mystery was written down in 1935, the legend comes from perhaps as much as a century earlier, documented on paper thanks again to the tireless efforts of Charles E. Brown. Mr. Brown had more than a penchant for folklore and became the first director of the Wisconsin State Historical Society back in 1908. Mr. Brown shared in one of his many published pamphlets a story of the Bear family. The Bears were a family from the Winnebago tribe. The family regularly spent time around what is now Lake Wingra on Madison's south side. They would camp there, hunt there, get fresh water from the springs there and trap game throughout the winter around the lake. They would bravely do all this, despite the belief by many in the tribe that a "big, wild animal lived in the lake." This was seemingly not an animal to be revered; rather, it was to be feared. It was described as having a "long tail and horns on its head." One Bear family member described an encounter with the creature.

Camped on the shores of Lake Wingra late one night, the family was awakened by a "terrible noise." There were other tribespeople camping in the area who also heard the commotion. It was described to sound like "sharp explosions, crashing sounds." The story says the noises "continued for a long time." No one dared venture out in the dead of night; instead, they welcomed the increased nerve provided by dawn. Several of the Winnebagos headed out with the sunrise and reported back a frightful scene. In Lake Wingra and up a small creek, the ice was broken—exploded out and onto the shore as if some huge creature had crashed through and thrashed its way up the frozen creek bed, sending huge ice chunks every

A view of South Madison in 1909. *WHS-36063.*

which way. The report from the braver of the bunch sent everyone packing. Was the experience in the middle of the night a fearful misunderstanding of a natural ice break? Did the frigid temperatures, wind and current patterns merely cause the ice to heave in some natural way? One can still see this occurrence on the larger lakes throughout Madison. On any given winter's day, huge sheets of ice break up and push above the normal ice layer and onto the shore. I would be less likely to discount the experience relayed to Mr. Brown by the Bear family, as they had spent much time in the wilds and in this specific area. They undoubtedly would have experienced the same ice cleavage every winter.

I have yet to meet someone who lives in the wilderness who does not hold a strong understanding of the natural ebb and flow of it. It has been my experience that those living in nature quickly learn to work with and around it rather than against it. Those who don't don't last long to explain why their way didn't work. I have a strong feeling that the Winnebagos would have appreciated their surroundings and found ways to enjoy the natural splendor that Madison held in the early 1800s. I also doubt very much that most of the more modern lake monster witnesses from the 1900s knew of the Bear family's experience. One thing is for certain: the sightings remain a mystery to this day. But if there were something that was unique enough to the area's people to earn a name, and their fear, what was it and where did it come from?

I've lived in Madison and the general Madison area for the majority of my short life. It wasn't until sitting down to write this book that I discovered the Madison lakes are basically connected to the world's oceans. Though I've never made the trip myself, here's how it is said to go: the Yahara River connects several of the Madison Lakes to the Rock River; the Rock connects to the Mississippi River; the Mississippi connects to the Gulf of Mexico; the Gulf connects to the Atlantic Ocean; and the Atlantic to— well, everything else! Now before you begin, yes, I understand there is saltwater biology versus freshwater and countless locks, shallows and bends between the ocean deeps and, say, Lake Mendota. There are still countless creatures we as humans have yet to discover living in the world's oceans. Even if they are not alive today, perhaps they were two hundred years ago when this legend may have originated. Some liberal estimates of the world's species extinction rate rise as high as twenty per day. Perhaps the creature the legend speaks of was the last of its kind. Of course, this is all speculation, based on potentials that are nearly incalculable, but it is fun to partake in nonetheless.

I have yet to find the original source material; however, it is claimed in several writings that Charles Brown came into the possession of a large and unidentified scale. It was said to have been found in one of the Madison Lakes. The year was 1917, and the story goes on to report that University of Wisconsin professors became involved in futile attempts to identify the scale. There have also been stories of large, mysterious skeletal remains found along the shores of Madison-area lakes. My investigations remain ongoing.

Bryant Road on Madison's south side was no place to be found after nightfall in the late 1800s. It was believed by many to be a haunted and cursed roadway. The thoroughfare even earned a few nicknames: "ghost walk" or "ghost road," depending on which area resident you talked to at the time. Whether on horseback, riding in a buggy or using your own two feet to brave the road, you were equally cursed to encounter something. In *Haunted Wisconsin*, the authors speak of how "most described the ghost as a luminous white vapor that would appear suddenly from the brush on either side of the road, follow the unsuspecting for a short distance, and then vanish as quickly as it had appeared." Others described being shadowed by a "Native American astride a pony" that would trail behind them and then mysteriously vanish. The farmers who lived along the road reported hearing unshod hooves, which could have given way to the indigenous Americans

A Seminole Highway sign marking the area where many unexplained reports once came from. *Photograph by Zach Boynton.*

theory. Even disembodied horse hoof beats were reported pounding down the roadway with nothing in sight but the still of night. Different sources have recounted unexplained globes of light that chased and teased early visitors up and down the fence line, inexplicably dancing about.

As stories age, details can be lost altogether or changed completely. With more than one hundred years of evolution, the experiences had along this old country lane that sat south of Madison have become cloudy. The Bryant family is said to have once owned land in the area of the road. Having a small family cemetery was not uncommon a century ago, and they were said to have buried a man near their barn, just off the roadway. A few believed this might have been the source of the specters seen in the night. Others speculated that a Native American warrior had never left and now sought revenge for his own untimely slaughter. For years as a child, I unknowingly passed through this once-cursed area. I have since returned to investigate the roadway over the last decade, seeking new clues to the old mystery. You will no longer find Bryant Road on any Madison maps. If you dare, you will keep reading to find the current name of this once haunted hallow. If you are brave, you will continue to use Seminole Highway.

From this same area comes yet another ghost story. This time, it involves a phantom woodcutter—or so the story goes. The families surrounding Noe Woods first conveyed the unexplained events. This story gained much attention, thanks to Beth Scott and Michael Norman in their haunted books. Sometime in the 1870s, this south side area went by the name of Bartlett's Woods. Farmer Albert Lamson's ears were cursed one night by a repetitive noise emanating from the nearby woods. It was the clear sound of an axe head whacking away at a tree. This sound would have been a distinctive one for a farmer in the 1800s. Albert was curious enough to head out into the woods, though he wisely waited until the next day. He was looking for where some stranger had chopped down a tree in the dark of night. He found no woodchips, no stump, no drag marks and no hoof marks—nothing but a mystery. Confounded, Albert inquired with his neighbors. His property bordered with Charley Nelson's, now the Arboretum Administration area and Curtis Prairie.

His neighbors did indeed describe hearing the same ominous chopping sound but had no earthly explanation for it. The phantom axe ringing in the night continued for months, until local curiosity grew to posse status. Area men armed with lanterns set out to discover the truth behind this mystery, leaving fear behind. Not far enough behind, however, as it is reported that at the last minute the search party hesitated and disbanded. As everyone left, the only thing that remained was the mystery of the phantom wood chopping that went on through the fall of that same year. With the fear too great for the local men to investigate, perhaps they simply stopped reporting it. After all, what would be the point of discussing it if embarrassment were the only thing ever discovered?

If you're looking for the opportunity to test your fortitude, what better place than an apple orchard on a cool summer's eve or a rolling pumpkin patch in the dusk of a brisk fall day. There just so happens to be both at Eplegaarden Orchard, located in the southern area of old Ghost Road. It welcomes you to take in the scenery, and possibly the spirits, of its more than one hundred sprawling acres. The website speaks of the possibility that the old barn and silo may have hauntings, especially when the west wind blows. In addition, the orchard has a plaque on its Sesquicentennial Barn from the Smithsonian Institution telling of its historic travels across the country.

A bit farther east of the Seminole Highway and the lumberjack-haunted woods is a lake that goes by the name Waubesa. This lake, like many others in the area, was once home to mysterious monsters from the deep. On August 22, 1899, Barney Reynolds was visiting from Illinois. He rowed a small boat out onto Lake Waubesa, hoping to have an enjoyable day of

The view that awaits you at Eplegaarden Orchard, near the end of old Ghost Road. *Photograph by Noah Voss.*

fishing. The lake was said to be very calm when all of a sudden the surface of the water a few hundred feet from him "began to heave and swell." From the boiling water came a huge body that he estimated to be sixty to seventy feet in length. The color of the creature was "dark green" and had a "serpent head" that he came face to face with. He felt threatened enough at that distance to row back to shore as quickly and quietly as he could.

As soon as Barney relayed his experience to others, his standing came under attack. It was said that he was not foreign to the bottle, and his integrity was questioned. Many disregarded the whole experience. That is, until a couple witnessed an unidentified creature swimming in the lake later that same summer. The husband and wife were just off Waubesa Beach when they saw the head of the lake monster surface. This time, the report indicated that the monster began moving directly toward the couple, who quickly swam to shore. The only other detail we have on record is how the eyes glistened. Thanks to Wisconsin historian Charles Brown, many of these initial reports have been reprinted in many sources until they reached these pages today.

Mr. Reynolds, our last witness, likely would have considered the time he was living in to be an exciting one. It was nearly New Year's celebration time by most people's standards, and just as today, 1899's hyped atmosphere was no different. The New Year's celebration parties were hurriedly being planned in every household; magazines and newspapers ran retrospections of the last one hundred years, as well as futuristic predictions for the next one hundred. Looking back, the last century was given many nicknames, such as "the wonderful century," "the people's century" and even "the era of astronomical discovery." Others, looking forward, were maybe more mundane. Optimism won out, and speculation that people would be taller and healthier and live longer in the next one hundred years ruled the conversations. The newer inventions of the time consisted of electricity in many new uses, the telephone, carbonated drinks and the phonograph. These were being shown off at the World's Fair, a cutting-edge expo of the time. Indeed, the first phone call to take place in Wisconsin happened in 1874. Though that call took place in Janesville, Madison's first call is thought to have been placed in 1878. Shortly after, a system was set up to display the new technology to Madison legislators. Lines were strung from the capitol to Science Hall for the calls. It was reported in the papers that the professors and legislators were so taken by the new technology that they talked all night.

Just as our modern-day New Year's celebrations bring out quotes and comments from celebrities, so too did those in 1899. Senator John Ingalls spoke of "the journey from New York City and San Francisco…[which] will be made between sunrise and sunset of a summer day." In his vision of the future, "it will be as common for the citizen to call for his dirigible balloon as it now is for his buggy and boots." Others, such as columnist Mary Lease, had visions even more grandiose: "We will hold communication with the inhabitants of other planets, and Sunday excursions to the mountains of the moon will not excite comment." I hope Mary was simply ahead of her time and a few years early on her estimate of first contact. Much of the speculation was to become fact. People of 1899 often cited the future as being full of fully electrified homes, heating and cooling that adjusted automatically throughout the day and seasons, radio, airliners and high-speed rails. Finally, New Year's Eve came.

At the stroke of midnight, celebrations peaked across the United States. In New York, electric lights were strung on invisible wires throughout the city. Chicago stores sold out of party supplies as revelers paraded up and down the streets blowing kazoos. In Los Angeles, cannons were shot off to ring in the New Year. Emile Zola, a forward-thinking writer, editorialized

The Lockheed T-33 Shooting Star jet trainer. *Image courtesy of the United States federal government.*

that the following one hundred years would hold evenly distributed wealth and the end to corruption, the exploitation of workers, the sick and the poor.

Only fifty-two years later, our next mystery brings about jet airplanes and investigators from Project Blue Book right here in Madison. While there were two witnesses to this next UFO, the additionally unique part is where they made their observations. United States Air Force Captain Bridges and First Lieutenant Johneon were in mid–jet training flights. They flew the T-33 Shooting Star.

The T-33 took first flight in 1948, and since then has been used by thirty different countries around the globe and is still in use today. At 5:45 p.m., the pilots' training flight took on a new twist as they reported "four bright lights, in a diamond formation." They turned their T-33 and gave chase, heading toward the objects now about ten miles south of Madison. Following procedure, the pilots requested a radar confirmation. Ground radar didn't have any other targets on their screen besides the T-33. Captain Bridges estimated the UFOs to be traveling at four hundred miles per hour and was able to overtake the formation of "white lights" in about five minutes' time. The UFOs stayed on a heading 130 degrees southwest and now were only ten miles northeast of Janesville, Wisconsin. As they neared Janesville, the UFOs' heading changed to an easterly one. The pilots continued their observations of the four UFOs as their fuel began running low. As the UFOs continued toward Milwaukee, the T-33 crew was documented as making one more observation. They described the UFOs as having no "silhouette visible even when the objects were seen against Milwaukee city lights." From the report, it seems as if the UFOs had no visible structure to them. Perhaps the structure was obscured by the light being produced or even reflected by the objects. Further speculation could even have the UFOs completely emanating light, making any description difficult. Of course, one could venture guesses that the UFOs had some form of cloaking technology—or no technology at all and were some natural occurrence such as plasma.

The T-33 crew was forced to turn back or risk running out of fuel. The entire event lasted only ten minutes. Even after the proceeding follow-up by investigators from Project Blue Book, the experience was labeled "Unknown." Already having touched upon the vast and complexly layered history of the United States federal government's involvement in UFO research, let's take a look at semantics. We know that at the time of this sighting, Project Blue Book was amidst management change and reorganization. Through its history, it held multiple definitions of and categories for experiences reported to it. From around that time, we have three main options that the investigators used to categorize the reports they researched. This was especially clear for those working on the statistical data for Project Blue Book Special Report No. 14.

First, we have *identified* defined as "sufficient specific information has been accumulated and evaluated to permit a positive identification or explanation of the object." The second category used was *insufficient information*, or sightings where "one or more elements of information essential for evaluation are missing." The third and final category was *unknown*: "a report apparently contains all pertinent data necessary to suggest a valid hypothesis concerning the cause or explanation of the report but the description of the object or its motion cannot be correlated with any known object or phenomena."

Most UFOlogists maintain that the insufficient information and identified categories were incorrectly combined to skew the statistical data for Special Report No. 14. What the intent was for doing this is unclear. The unknown cases in Wisconsin alone range from fifteen to as many as twenty-six reports. The discrepancy comes from the evolving status of categories, techniques and prerogatives of those in charge. Before we leave the UFO topic, let's look at some intriguing findings from Special Report No. 14. Of the main categories for UFO sightings, there were many subcategories. The ones we are interested in right now are only two. One was "excellent" and the other "poorest." Simply put, the excellent stack of sightings had sufficient information gathered that the reviewers felt could warrant further scrutiny and potentially hold pertinent information. Of the thirty-two hundred reports reviewed by Special Report No. 14, a full 35 percent of the excellent pile was categorized as unknown. By contrast, the poorest of reports contained only 18 percent unknown. This runs contradictory to what was publicly expected and put forward. Many people to this day still believe that the vast majority of, if not all, UFO sightings are misidentifications and with more information could simply be identified—or are from crackpots, which numbered only 1.5 percent of all cases reviewed in Special Report No. 14. (Yes, they had a category for that, too.) This special report focused only on sightings collected from 1947 through 1954. In a few short years, with very limited resources, I have been able to receive and archive over one thousand UFO reports on my single website: UFOwisconsin.com.

Collecting insufficient amounts of quantifiable data from experiencers of the unexplained plagues the field of research to this day. The main cause, as most see it, is proper resources, which endeavors like Project Blue Book had at times overcome.

Our next mystery begins above southern Madison and ends devastatingly quick. The year 1953 brought a mysterious loss of life to the 433rd Fighter Interceptor Squadron normally stationed in Madison at the Truax Air Field. The 433rd had a detachment of two F-89 Scorpion Jet Interceptors located at Kinross, Michigan. Kinross houses a small military base that juts out into Lake Superior, nearing the Canadian border. As with any good story, let's start at the beginning. We don't have to go back any further than six hours before two F-89s are dispatched from Michigan to intercept an unknown return showing on radar scopes. This radar return remains a UFO to this day.

Back in Madison, the time was approximately 12:45 p.m. on November 23. People were out and about enjoying an average fall day. Both men aboard another F-89 Jet Interceptor were World War II veteran pilots. Their short mission on this day was to test out the new J-35-A-47 engines attached to their Scorpion fighter jet.

Afterburners fired as they rapidly climbed to an altitude of forty thousand feet, "broadcasting performance data to the ground recording unit." The tests on the new engines were complete. They radioed the mission objective reached and the new course vectoring them back to Truax Air Field.

An F-89 Jet Interceptor stationed at Madison Truax Air Field, Wisconsin. *Image courtesy of the United States federal government.*

This facility is located on the northeast side of Madison and is now more commonly referred to as Dane County Regional Airport.

The next thing we know comes from eyewitnesses near the Arboretum Park located just a bit south of the capitol building. Mrs. Donald A. was standing just outside her Madison home when she suddenly "saw a jet overhead." She reported to the newspapers that "the jet then plummeted to earth—just so fast your eye could hardly follow it." She went on to say that "it was quite low and I knew it was a jet, but there wasn't any noise like you always hear from a jet. It was just still-like...suddenly there was something just like an explosion—oh, an awful, huge noise." One other reporting witness recalled, "I heard the plane roaring across the hill and thought it was going to land in the marsh south of my house." A witness approximately two miles from the crash site recounted, "Then it pulled up...lifted up over and headed for the arboretum." Just before it disappeared from sight, "there was a puff of smoke and the plane seemed to dive right straight down." Tragically, after that, "there was a real loud thud and I knew it had crashed."

Wisconsin State Journal

Pair Goes Down with Craft

2 TRUAX MEN KILLE
IN JET'S CRASH HER

Rescue Squad Probes Watery Hole Where Plane Crashed

Mechanical Faul
Believed to Blam

Victim's Family Waits

Many Watch, Hear Plane's Death Dive

*dget Board Drops Golf Course
nd, Asks No Tax Rate Increase*

*Jet That Crashed Here W
'Corrected' Model, Shoup S*

The front page of a newspaper detailing the F-89's deadly descent into the Arboretum. *Image courtesy of the* Wisconsin State Journal, *November 23, 1953.*

Approximately six hours later, several hundred miles to the north, there were two additional F-89s, stationed there temporarily from the Madison Truax Air Field on border alert patrol. Their main function was to take flight at a moment's notice to intercept, identify and neutralize any threats to the United States. One such threat was detected on radar. The pair of jets scrambled; their target was 160 miles northwest of their location, and they raced forward at over five hundred miles per hour. Revealing one very good reason to send aircraft on these important missions in pairs, the second F-89 encountered mechanical problems not long into the flight and had to turn around, returning safely to base. Shortly after, the two radar returns became one. They were approximately 70 miles out over Lake Superior at the time. The radar controller was not able to raise the crew of the F-89. Fearing the worst, search and rescue were scrambled. The original UFO on the radar screen continued on its course. The F-89 and its crew were never recovered.

Pilots Lieutenant Felix Moncla and Second Lieutenant Robert Wilson, normally stationed out of Madison, were presumed dead. There have been several official and unnofficial theories put forward. However, for most UFOlogists and some family members, it remains a mystery.

Conclusion

Mysteries, untold secrets, enigmatic experiences, cryptic anything—all of this holds an aura of action for me. It makes me feel that someone is obscuring the truth, hiding the next clue or sending me down a path with no answers. There is almost an intelligent intent behind it, thumbing its nose. It drives me. Not crazy, but it motivates me to learn more. The feeling that a mystery is unsolved makes me want to find the solution. Perhaps at one point in my life I may have conceded that not all answers were obtainable. I certainly don't feel that way now. Though I doubt there is always intent or intelligence behind a mystery, there is a draw to the inexplicable that fires something in the brain of those with more curiosity than stress. If answers were not forthcoming in a mystery, I would suspect that in time, they would be. Some cases will grow cold, and the data to solve them will be lost. The new mysteries—those not yet born in either action or plan—will be less likely to remain in the comfort of obscurity.

The mystery waiting to be discovered holds an arcane connection to the past. These mysteries are out there, waiting to be uncovered. The mystery forgotten has lost its immortality unless someone—anyone—learns what once was. I truly hope the unexplained contained in *Mysterious Madison* motivates you to enjoyment or to action. Whether your enjoyment is in fear, repulsion or intrigue, there are many more mysteries that I couldn't fit in these pages. Maybe you'll find your next road trip destination in this book? The bolder among us may use these cases as a stepping-off point to find the next unknown mystery already out there, waiting to be discovered, researched, explored and maybe even solved!

Find your motivation. Remember, adventures come to the adventuresome.

WORKS CONSULTED

Allen, Robert S. "Marveling at Mystery of Lakes, Pioneer Passes On." January 20, 1922.

Balousek, Marv. "Body of Murder Victim Exhumed." *Wisconsin State Journal*, November 3, 1982.

———. "Few Leads in Murder." *Wisconsin State Journal*, July 3, 1982.

———. "Holiday Hampers Murder Probe." *Wisconsin State Journal*, July 4, 1982.

———. *101 Wisconsin Unsolved Mysteries*. N.p.: Badger Books Inc, 2000.

Birmingham, Robert A., and Leslie E. Eisenberg. *Indian Mounds of Wisconsin*. Madison: University of Wisconsin Press, 2000.

Capital Times. "Gangland's Guns, Silent for Two Years, Bark Again: Italian Killed." April 10, 1928.

———. "Italian Leader Murdered In 'Rum Feud.'" March 17, 1924.

———. "Italian Leader Slain: Two Held." April 10, 1928.

———. "Lemberger Is Held." October 5, 1921.

———. "Saturday 10th Anniversary of Murder of Patrolman; Still Mystery." February 1, 1928.

———. "Sober Witness Describes UFO." November 21, 1985.

Cass, Betty. "Smallest Doll in World Is Owned by Engineer Student." *Wisconsin State Journal*, October 1, 1922.

Coyle, Owen. "Seek Help of Family in Hunt for Murderer." *Capital Times*, May 28, 1968.

Dawson, William M. "Justo Victim of Bandit Revenge." *Capital Times*, February 14, 1922.

Department of Natural Resources. http://dnr.wi.gov/org/land/er/mammals/cougar/sightings.htm.

Doehlert, Betsy. "Do Ghosts Walk the Arboretum Glades?" *Capital Times*, October 31, 1977.

Durrie, Daniel S. *A History of Madison, The Capital of Wisconsin; Including the Four Lake Country*. N.p.: Atwood & Culver, 1874.

Godfrey, Linda S. *Strange Wisconsin: More Badger State Weirdness*. Trails Books, 2007.

Hall, Michael David. *UFOs: A Century of Sightings*. Galde Press Inc, 1999.

Knudson, Willard G. "Thanksgiving Day First Observed Here in 1838." *Wisconsin State Journal*, November 26, 1930.

Lewis, Chad. *The Hidden Headlines of Wisconsin*. Madison, WI: Unexplained Research Publishing Company, 2007.

———. *The Road Guide to Wisconsin's Mysterious Creatures*. N.p.: On the Road Publications, 2011.

Madison, Dane County and Surrounding Towns. N.p.: WM. J. Park & Co., 1877.

Madison Democrat. "New Year's In '51." December 31, 1899.

New York Times. "Child-Slayer Confesses." September 14, 1911.

———. "Lemberger Denies Killing Daughter." October 7, 1921.

Norman, Michael, and Beth Scott. *Haunted Wisconsin*. N.p.: Trails Books, 2001.

Oshkosh Northwestern. "Quaint Tales Handed Down By Winnebago." July 14, 1927.

Peterson, Gary. "Picnic Point: Witches Wail, Sea Serpents Slurp?" *Capital Times*, October 26, 1978.

Rath, Jay. "Bascom Hill: Old Haunt or Still Haunted?" *Wisconsin State Journal*, October 24, 1988.

———. *The W-Files True Reports of Wisconsin's Unexplained Phenomena*. N.p.: Trails Books, 1997.

Scott, Beth, and Michael Norman. *True Ghost Stories: Haunted Heartland from the American Midwest*. N.p.: Barnes and Noble Books, 1985.

Strub, Sherry. *Ghosts of Madison*. N.p.: Schiffer, 2008.

Surrounded By Reality. http://www.surroundedbyreality.com.

UFO Wisconsin. http://www.UFOwisconsin.com.

Unexplained Research. http://www.UnexplainedResearch.com.

Voss, Noah. *UFO Wisconsin: A Progress Report*. Madison, WI: Unexplained Research Publishing Company, 2008.

Waukesha Daily Freeman. "Suspect Found With Gun Used To Kill Cop." December 3, 1924.

The W-Files. http://www.W-Files.com.

Wisconsin History. https://www.wisconsinhistory.org.

Wisconsin State Journal. "The Fiend Must Be Found." September 9, 1911.

————. "Find No Trace of Kidnapped Child." September 7, 1911.

————. "Lembergers Are Subpoenaed To Appear At Coroner's Inquest." September 11, 1911.

————. "Little Girl Is Kidnapped." September 11, 1911.

————. "Scientist Was Nearing Solution of Mystery, Nature of Energy Transfer, Colleagues Believe." July 2, 1931.

————. "Squads Seek Clues in Justl's Murder." December 8, 1972.

————. "Warrant Is Asked for Johnson." September 11, 1911.

About the Author

Noah keeps busy running his numerous websites: GetGhostGear.com, where he was the first in the world to exclusively offer paranormal investigating equipment for sale around the globe; UFOwisconsin.com, where he regularly posts new reports on Wisconsin's UFO phenomenon, with over one thousand archived reports; and W-Files.com, running all things odd since it was first published in 1997.

Beyond publishing over four thousand web pages, Noah authored *UFO Wisconsin: A Progress Report* in 2008 detailing over one hundred reports of UFOs in a nonfiction, Wisconsin-based book published by Unexplained Research Publishing Company. Noah has worked with such companies as the History Channel, the SyFy Channel, the CW Network, Triage Entertainment and Lions Gate Films on projects ranging from UFO documentaries to ABC's *Scariest Places on Earth*. From 2005 through 2008, Noah was a regular keynote speaker with the Unexplained Conferences, the longest-running paranormal program of its kind in the world and the largest in America. Noah has appeared in print, on radio and on television in over forty countries.

Noah has travelled throughout most states in America—researching ghostly St. Augustine, Florida; investigating the mysterious Winchester Mansion in California; going for the gone at the Bennington Black Hole in Vermont; driving the haunted highways in Hawaii; looking for Bessie in Lake Erie; trying to get lost in the Bridgewater Triangle of Massachusetts; scanning for flying saucers on the summit of Mount Saint Helens; searching for werewolves in Wisconsin and the ghosts of Alcatraz in San Francisco Bay; exploring the Historic Bullock Hotel of Wild West Deadwood; investigating the mystery of the Paulding Lights of Michigan; looking for what went wrong in Salem, Massachusetts; prying for Pepie in Lake Pepin on the Mississippi; flying through the Bermuda Triangle; practicing voodoo in Jamaica; spotting UFOs in Mexico; and searching for sasquatch in British Columbia.